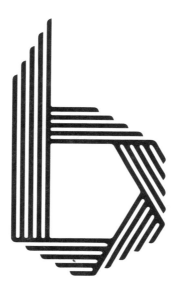

BANDING TOGETHER

A **Practical Guide** for **Disciple Makers**

JON WIEST

LEADER'S GUIDE

wesleyan
PUBLISHING HOUSE
wphstore.com
Indianapolis, Indiana

Copyright © 2018 by Jon Wiest
Published by Wesleyan Publishing House
Indianapolis, Indiana 46250
Printed in the United States of America
ISBN: 978-1-63257-267-7
ISBN (e-book): 978-1-63257-268-4

Are you looking for a historically-rooted, culturally-relevant, and applicable pathway of discipleship that leads to multiplication? Look no further. In *Banding Together*, Jon Wiest doesn't hold back from sharing his practical experiences of leading a disciple-making movement within the framework of a local church. He not only convinces you that Jesus' mandate of disciples making disciples is essential, but also shows a simple scaffold for implementation with the people God has entrusted to you. *Banding Together* will inspire, challenge, and help you lead a disciple-making movement that will lead to exponential fruitfulness in the kingdom of God.

—Ed Love, director of church multiplication for The Wesleyan Church

It's an easy read—simple, short, and practical—but its impact will be catalytic in starting a much-needed movement across the church. Wiest has recaptured the genius of Wesley's strategy for revival which is found, not in the clergy, but in the laity, and not only in his preaching, but in his small bands. As I read Wiest's book, I see how my own preaching over the years would have been more powerful under the guidance of these principles. Nevertheless, I'm excited about the big influence this little book will have on the church, with the result that many people who were once only "saved," will actually be converted by the power of God's Spirit unleashed through God's Word. These principles have already helped our church and they will help in yours.

—Steve DeNeff, lead pastor of College Church (Marion, Indiana)

Jon has written a simple, practical, and compelling approach to making disciples that can be easily implemented by your organization. I believe in this approach and have seen it work first hand in my church, in my discipleship group, and in the significant impact on my own spiritual journey. This has been one of the best ideas our local church has utilized in a long time, getting us to focus once again on regularly reading God's Word and applying it in practical ways to our lives. I am of the firm opinion that many churches and their constituents could benefit by following these principles and this plan for "making disciples who make disciples."

—Carl L. Shepherd, board chair, Indiana Wesleyan University

We tend to over-complicate disciple making and church multiplication. Jon Wiest brings the antidote to our poison with this clear, concrete guide. He'll walk you through convictions and practicalities that can turn your single congregation into a small movement of churches. I've been doing this a long time, but this book showed me two options I had long overlooked.

—Ralph Moore, founder of Hope Chapel Churches

Banding Together is written out of experience and results. There are many testimonies of bolder, more courageous and loving Christ followers who are continuing the journey of *Banding Together* in recent years. However, this is also based on several hundreds of years of practice resulting in transformation of people, communities, and nations. I like to imagine all God wants to do through the practice of this simple, yet profound, book.

—Jo Anne Lyon, Ambassador, General Superintendent Emerita of The Wesleyan Church

Pastor Jon's new discipleship material is tried and true. He has implemented this program into his local church setting and this program has turned into a movement! The plan has three simple elements; Scripture, the Spirit, and community. All three mingle together beautifully into life transformation for believers of all ages. This material for leaders is theologically grounded in the Wesleyan tradition yet welcoming to folks from all Christian denominations. Every place I travel and teach, I highly recommend this book to start (or jump-start) a church's Bible reading program.

—Dave Smith, pastor of ministry development and teaching, pastor at College Church (Marion, Indiana), and church ambassador and professor of Bible at Indiana Wesleyan University

To my friend, Mike Colaw, and the many discipleship group leaders at Trinity Church. This book is the fruit of your dedication to disciple making.

CONTENTS

INTRODUCTION
DISCIPLE MAKING

"Therefore go and make disciples." (Matt. 28:19)

How would you react if someone you loved returned from the dead to give you a special assignment? How well would you listen? How intently would you follow their commands?[1] I suspect that such an extraordinary experience would be met with absolute obedience and alter the trajectory of your life.

This scenario is not hypothetical—it happened. Jesus rose from the dead and gave the command known as the Great Commission. His words were clear: "All authority in heaven and on earth has been given to me. Therefore go and make disciples" (Matt. 28:18–19). Go and make disciples! Along with the command to love God and love others, these are the basic instructions of the Christian life (see 22:37–39).

Love God. Love Others. Make Disciples.

This is the operating system for every church and follower of Christ. Without it running in the background, nothing else matters. Worship gatherings, ministry programs, small-group studies, and outreach events that aren't making disciples fall short. So let me ask, are you making disciples?

I've discovered in twenty years of ministry that the challenge is not convincing people of the importance of disciple making—it's explaining a clear process for getting the job done. How do you make disciples? This brief guide answers that question.

My goal is to present a simple, practical, biblical strategy for group discipleship that leads to multiplication. It's a strategy that will help you and your church take the first steps toward making and multiplying disciples in your context, with roots in one of the greatest disciple-making movements in history.

Sustaining a Movement

George Whitefield was Methodism's first and most popular spokesperson. His first open-air sermon was on February 17, 1739, and by his own estimates, he gave at least 18,000 sermons in his lifetime. He preached more hours a day than he slept. More than ten million people on two continents are said to have heard his message. Whitefield was instrumental in the Great Awakening of Britain and the American colonies, making seven trips across the Atlantic to preach in America. Benjamin Franklin, one of Whitefield's admirers, devised an experiment proving that Whitefield standing in open space could easily address 30,000 people at a time. Eyewitnesses said his voice could be heard up to two miles away.[2] George Whitefield was one of the most prolific and powerful evangelists of all time.

Whitefield's passion for the lost ran high, and in 1770, the fifty-five-year-old made the famous statement, "I had rather wear out than rust out."[3] This statement would prove prophetic. The next day, after preaching a rousing sermon, George Whitefield died. Many would say the revival died with him. The movement ended, but another movement continued.

The Wesleyan movement began under the leadership of John and Charles Wesley and was carried over to the American colonies by Francis Asbury. Asbury is widely considered to be the father of early American Methodism, and like Whitefield, Asbury had great determination and drive. Estimates say he traveled over 130,000 miles on horseback, crossed the Allegheny Mountains sixty times, visited every state in the union once a year, and rose at 4:00 each morning to spend at least an hour or two in prayer. He preached more than 10,000 sermons and ordained upwards of 3,000 preachers.[4]

Asbury achieved for Methodism what can only be called a miracle of growth, launching the movement from a few hundred individuals in 1770, to nearly 500,000 members and 6,000,000 people fifty years later.[5] It is no stretch to say that the early American Methodist movement was the greatest disciple-making, church-planting movement in the history of the United States, thriving long after Asbury's death.

What was the difference? Why did Whitefield's revival end with his death, while the Wesleyan revival continued to thrive long after the death of its founder? The answer is found in Wesley's simple discipleship strategy of societies (large group gatherings), classes (small group gatherings), and band meetings (groups of three to five). Adam Clark, an early historian of Methodism, commented:

> It was by this means [the formation of Societies] that we have been enabled to establish permanent and holy churches over the world. Mr. Wesley saw the necessity of this from the beginning. Mr. Whitefield, when he separated from Mr. Wesley, did not follow it. What was the consequence? The fruit of Mr. Whitefield died with himself. Mr. Wesley's fruit remains, grows, increases, and multiplies exceedingly.[6]

Whitefield himself is said to have confessed to an old friend later in life, "My brother Wesley acted wisely; the souls that were awakened under his ministry he joined in class, and thus preserved the fruits of his labor. This I neglected, and my people are a rope of sand."[7]

Whitefield was a passionate evangelist who proclaimed the gospel to everyone he met. Wesley realized that, while evangelism was essential, sustaining a movement required making disciples. In fact, Wesley felt so strongly about disciple making that he would not send preachers where he couldn't follow up with discipleship. Failure to support new believers was, in his words, "begetting children for the murderer."[8] Wesley wrote, "Establish class meetings and form societies wherever you preach and have attentive hearers . . . for wherever we have preached without doing this, the word has been like seed sown by the wayside."[9] These are words we need to consider.

The revival ended. A rope of sand. Seed sown by the wayside.

Wesley's genius, and the main reason we remember him, is in his blueprint that ensured Methodists would become faithful disciples of Jesus. This emphasis on intentional disciple making has been a hallmark, sustaining all the great movements of God. The early church, Celtic missions, Moravians, Methodists, Pentecostals, Chinese house churches, and twenty-first century awakenings have all had an intentional focus on obedience-based, group discipleship.[10]

It is also the focus of this book. If we want to see a movement that lasts, we must get intentional about making disciples.

A Multiplication Strategy

I reference John Wesley and his methods throughout this book primarily because he is one of my disciple-making heroes. I am also part of the Wesleyan tribe. Recently, our leadership laid out the goal of "celebrating every time a disciple makes a disciple and a church multiplies itself until there is a transforming presence in every ZIP code."[11]

There is an implied progression to that vision. It begins with disciples making disciples and continues with churches planting churches. If you make disciples, you will always have a church, but if you plant a church, you may not always make disciples.[12] Disciple making is the critical engine for multiplication. Only a strong wave of disciple making can provide the raw material for starting new congregations and multiplying churches.

Consider the difference. Church A has developed a ministry strategy around evangelism. It is a strategy of addition. They deeply desire to see people come to Christ and their plan is to grow increasingly larger through the primary draw of weekend worship services and creative programming. They are doing a fantastic job. They planted the church ten years ago and each year they have grown by almost one hundred people. In ten years, this high growth rate has resulted in many new believers and a church of almost one thousand in weekend attendance. Church A has quickly become a church of influence with an amazing cast of leaders, but their focus has never been on disciple making. They now seem to be hitting a lid. New growth requires even higher capacity leaders, higher quality services, better programming, and more streamlined systems to manage the crowds. While lay leaders have been equipped to bring friends and even share their faith, they aren't equipped to make disciples, and the growth of the church has slowed.

Church B has developed a ministry strategy around disciple making. It is a strategy of multiplication. Their plan is to grow through a firm commitment to making disciples and developing leaders. In the first year, the founding pastor does nothing more than invest in disciple-making activities with a few trusted friends, modeling the process of discipleship. He or she decides to put in place a practical system whereby each person is asked to make three disciples every year and then encourages those disciples to do the same. This slow-moving discipleship ministry creeps forward with only the pastor and three others being impacted in the entire first year. Compared to Church A's growth, Church B's could easily seem discouraging. In fact, by the third year, Church B has only multiplied to twenty-seven people, and the pastor realizes he will probably need to be bi-vocational. But the commitment to discipleship is strong, and the church presses forward. By year five, the church has multiplied to approximately two hundred and forty disciples making disciples, and excitement is beginning to grow. Weekend services are finally launched, but the primary driver and focus of the church's time, energy, and resources is discipleship. How large would this church be in ten years if they continued to multiply exponentially?

60,000 people.[13]

Let that number sink in for a moment—60,000 disciples who are now unleashed to impact their world for Christ. That type of church will require a different kind of leadership and focus than Church A, but the result could be a disciple-making, church-multiplying, zip-code-changing movement. Whether those 60,000 gather regularly in a stadium or in thousands of homes around the city is beside the point. The point is the difference a focus on disciple making can have for the church.

Making disciples must be a core strategy for any multiplication movement.

A Practical Guide Is Needed

If the final words of the resurrected Christ are to go and make disciples, if his favor has been poured out on disciple-making movements around the world and throughout history, and if we are convinced of the multiplying power of disciple making, then why do so many individuals and churches struggle with getting the job done? To answer that question, I'd like to share an example from my own ministry.

God allowed me to have a part in planting two thriving churches over the course of ten years. Until a few years ago, I was convinced both churches were being obedient to the Great Commission. My philosophy of ministry was closer to Church A, and I had always interpreted the Great Commission as an evangelistic strategy. For me, church planting was about reaching the lost with the gospel. I prioritized the first half of the commission that talks about "baptizing them in the name of the Father and of the Son and of the Holy Spirit" (Matt. 28:19) and often neglected the second, "teaching them to obey everything I have commanded you" (v. 20). I wanted to grow the church so that we could plant other churches and establish a network of churches in our community. But over time, I began to put my trust in church growth principles and measure success on the metrics of attendance, professions of faith, and baptisms—to the neglect of making disciples and leading people into obedience. In my zeal to grow the church, win converts, and plant new churches, I lost my focus on discipleship.

Eventually, though, God got my attention. It came in the form of burnout followed by a three-month sabbatical. C. S. Lewis said that God "whispers to us in our pleasures . . . but shouts in our pain,"[14] and this was no exception. During my sabbatical, I saw that my philosophy of ministry was unbalanced and something was off in my approach. I had sacrificed disciple making at the altar of church growth and addition-oriented, evangelistic strategies. I had failed to pursue biblical disciple making as the mission of the church. I needed to repent.

But repentance wasn't enough. I also needed a clear strategy for making reproducing disciples. Now that my heart was open to discipleship, I needed the tools to make it happen. I knew how to gather people, preach inspiring messages, and plan meaningful worship services. I understood how to launch programs for children and students, and even offer small groups and classes for adults. However, I lacked a clear process for making disciples who could make disciples of others.

This desire for a practical, reproducing, disciple-making strategy is the basis for this book. In these pages, you will learn not only how to make disciples, but also how to multiply them. This model can be integrated into the disciple-making strategy of your church or personal life. It is also easily reproducible.

Finally, I need to make a confession. I've been hesitant to put this process into print. We are at the beginning of a journey to make discipleship the main engine of multiplication in our church, and by no means do we have everything figured out. There are many more conversations that need to take place around these issues, and clearly there are other strategies and models for making reproducing disciples. But we need to begin the dialogue.

I am convinced there is a growing group of pastors and lay leaders who are restless and hungry for something more than what they are currently experiencing. There are growing numbers of pastors and lay leaders realizing that Church

A strategies won't produce the fruit of Church B. Addition-oriented strategies are different than strategies of multiplication. The good news is that God has given you the capacity for this type of multiplication movement.

It begins with understanding a basic framework for disciple making in Part One, continues with implementing a simple process for group discipleship in Part Two, and concludes by lifting your eyes to the possibilities of launching an even greater disciple-making movement in Part Three.

There is a reason this book is described as a practical guide. The word *practical* means "concerned with the actual doing or use of something rather than with theory and ideas."[15] The purpose of this book isn't simply to get you *thinking* about making disciples. It's designed to push you forward and assist you in the *process* of making it happen.

PART ONE

THE **FRAMEWORK**

Basic convictions must be understood and established.

Vince Lombardi, the legendary American football coach of the Green Bay Packers, began each new season's training camp by pulling his team together, holding up a football, and saying, "Gentlemen . . . this is a football."[1] He would then walk his players out to the football field to show them the sidelines, hash marks, goal posts, and end zones. Finally, he would define for his players the goal of the game—to score more points than their opponent. Practice would then commence with blocking and tackling drills.

Basic stuff, to be sure.

Lombardi's focus on the fundamentals paid off. In nine years of coaching, his football teams played in the championship game every year but one, and his 1966-67 team won the very first Super Bowl, defeating the Kansas City Chiefs 35–10.[2] Lombardi understood that success in the game of football depended on learning and executing the fundamentals.

Disciple making is no different. We need to begin by establishing the fundamentals and framework for making disciples. In Part One of this book, we will organize this framework around five basic convictions. These five convictions serve the same purpose as Lombardi's "this is a football" speech. They will guide the rest of the book and give focus to our efforts.

CONVICTION #1
THE **PROCESS** IS **SIMPLE**

Simple is reproducible.

It's not enough to make disciples. Our goal is to make disciples who go out and make disciples of others. While sitting in a prison cell near the end of his life, the apostle Paul told his disciple Timothy, "And the things you have heard me say in the presence of many witnesses entrust to reliable people who will also be qualified to teach others" (2 Tim. 2:2). Paul invested in Timothy so that Timothy could invest in reliable people so that reliable people could be qualified to teach others. This is movement-oriented thinking through four generations. It also underlines the result of biblical disciple making: reproduction.

The more complicated the process, the more difficult it will be to reproduce. I know this from experience. Early on in ministry, I remember asking my pastor for tools to disciple a new believer named Ben. My pastor suggested taking Ben through the church's ten-week Theology 101 class and following up with a series of six-week curriculum options that a popular publishing house had recently released. This extended classroom and curriculum-based approach to discipleship required a master-level theology teacher, four workbooks, four separate study guides, and several trips to the local Christian bookstore. I slogged my way through nearly six months of meeting with my new disciple only to have him ask at the end of our time together, "Now what?"

Good question.

Nothing about this intensive discipleship process was easily reproducible. Ben didn't have the knowledge or teaching skills to duplicate a ten-week Theology 101 class for someone else. He wasn't equipped to wade through the curriculum options I had selected. As a college student, he couldn't invest nearly one hundred dollars to purchase a set of leader and participant guides for another disciple. By overcomplicating the process of disciple making, I had inadvertently stunted multiplication. Ben felt like disciple making was reserved for trained professionals. It wasn't simple enough. No wonder we often hear the following statements in our churches:

"I could never disciple someone."
"I wouldn't know where to start."
"I don't know enough about the Bible to help
    someone else."
"It all seems too complicated."

I recently received the latest discipleship curriculum from a leading Christian ministry that boasted four volumes with thirteen lessons each and an "easy pathway" for making disciples. Not exactly the simple process I had in mind.

One of my favorite movies is *Remember the Titans*. Denzel Washington plays an American high school football coach named Herman Boone, and in one scene, he reveals his playbook, which consists of six "split veer" running plays, to the coaching staff. One of the assistant coaches says, "Awful skinny playbook, ain't it coach?" Coach Boone fires back, "I run six plays, split veer. It's like Novocain. Just give it time, always works."[3] Coach Boone takes the next few months of practice working his players to the point that they can execute each of his six plays with perfection. The playbook was simple. The players responded, and the result was a state championship.

While making disciples requires great intentionality and hard work, a simple playbook allows us to give greater focus to our energy and efforts. Remember, if it's not simple, it won't be reproducible, and if it's not reproducible, there will be no movement. If making disciples requires long training sessions, stacks of curriculum options, massive amounts of preparation, and loads of administration, the movement will stall. The end goal is not to make a solitary disciple. The end goal is to launch a disciple-making movement.

The process must be simple.

CONVICTION #2
THE **CURRICULUM** IS THE **BIBLE**

Speaking of simplicity, what is often the most complicated part of discipleship? Choosing the right curriculum. With thousands of options available, wouldn't it be nice if someone could cut through the stacks of curricula to curate only the best resources for making disciples? Even better, what if Jesus could navigate our online retailers to guide us in picking out the perfect, God-inspired, silver-bullet, mother-of-all curriculum?

I think I know the book he would choose.

It is the only book on the market that is inspired by God (see 2 Tim. 3:16). The B-I-B-L-E. Maybe you remember the rest of the old Sunday school song, "Yes, that's the book for me; I stand alone on the Word of God. The B-I-B-L-E." It is the only curriculum that is inspired by God, will never run out of material, and will never run dry. We want people to engage directly with the Bible and hear directly from the Holy Spirit.

The reason I use the Bible as a disciple-making guide is because it is "God-breathed" and useful for "training in righteousness," as the apostle Paul said. Find the translation that best suits the people you are discipling and get started. I also recommend a reading plan. The Bible contains sixty-six books. Without a good reading plan or road map, it can be a difficult resource to navigate.

I once heard a story about a preacher whose car broke down on the side of a country road. He walked to a nearby road-house to use the phone and spotted Frank, an old friend and prominent businessman in the community. Frank was drunk, disheveled, and sitting at the bar. "What happened to you, Frank?" asked the good reverend. Frank told a sad tale of bad investments and deep debt. He wasn't sure how much longer he could outrun his creditors. The preacher had some advice. "Frank, I have so much confidence in God's Word that I want you to go home, open your Bible at random, stick your finger on a page, and I promise you that God will answer." Frank did what he was told.

One week later the pastor called Frank to check in on him, and Frank was elated. "Pastor, I found an answer to my problems, and I owe it all to you. I opened my Bible just like you said, put my finger down on the page, and there it was right in front of my eyes."

"What was the verse, Frank?" asked the preacher. "What did God say to get you out of debt and bring you such freedom?"

"Well, it wasn't actually a verse," said Frank. "I opened the Bible, and right there in front of my eyes was the answer . . . chapter 11. I filed for bankruptcy just yesterday. Thanks, pastor!"

You may laugh, but this is too often the approach people take when reading the Bible. Many new believers and even older Christians approach Scripture without a plan. They randomly open their Bible, read a few chapters, put it down, and immediately forget what they have read. Helping people navigate their time in God's Word is very important, and a reading plan is vital. In the next section, we look at a highly recommended reading plan that offers some more direction.

There is a promise in Scripture that affirms this second conviction. By studying God's Word, "the servant of God may be thoroughly equipped for every good work" (2 Tim. 3:17). I have found that when Christians spend a majority of their time on curriculum-based studies, they become dependent on those resources.[4] I prefer that followers of Christ become dependent on God's Word. No other curriculum is required.

The process is simple. The Bible is the curriculum.

CONVICTION #3
THE **TEACHER** IS THE **HOLY SPIRIT**

Who was your favorite teacher in high school or college?

Mine was Dr. Noll, my history professor at Wheaton College. Dr. Noll was intelligent, engaging, scholarly, well-spoken, and well-read. I sat in his lectures each week, mesmerized by his vast knowledge of history, theology, and the Bible. I also walked away from each class session thinking to myself, "I will never be that smart." As the semester went on, I became more and more convinced that I wouldn't pursue a PhD. I felt underqualified and less than brilliant compared to my professor. I wonder if many of us feel the same way when it comes to making disciples.

Underqualified. Intimidated. Overwhelmed.

Let me remove some of the pressure. In the disciple-making process, you don't need to have the answer to every question, prepare a lesson each week, or be a master-level teacher. In fact, the primary teacher is not you. The teacher is the Holy Spirit.

Your job is to help your disciples learn to listen to the Holy Spirit so they can learn how to trust and follow him. The Holy Spirit is the one who has promised to convict people of sin, lead them into righteousness, and guide them into all the truth (see John 16:13). He is the one who will reveal the truth of Scripture to them. He is the one who will soften their hearts and lead them to obedience.

Let me say it again: the teacher is the Holy Spirit. You are simply a conduit, a facilitator, and a channel for the Holy Spirit to work. It's not necessary for disciple makers to be seminary trained. Instead, the greater requirement is that they are sensitive to the Holy Spirit and willing to lean on him in the process. Certainly, biblical understanding and a growing relationship with Christ are important in making disciples, and there will often be need for solid biblical instruction. However, our primary job is to help others know how to listen to and hear from the Spirit.

Maybe you've heard the popular quote, "Give a man a fish and you feed him for a day. Teach a man to fish and you feed him for a lifetime." The same is true when it comes to disciple making. In showing others how to read God's Word and hear from the Holy Spirit, we are helping them learn how to spiritually feed themselves, facilitating a lifetime of growth.

Wayne Cordeiro, founding pastor of New Life Church in Honolulu, Hawaii, once told a story of a young staff member who decided to leave the church because he wasn't being spiritually fed. Cordeiro responded:

Imagine that my wife sees me one day, gaunt and emaciated. My eyes are sunken into gray sockets; my body is frail, exposing my skeleton; my abdomen is distended from starvation. I've obviously not been eating. When she sees me in this condition, she exclaims, "What in the world is happening to you?!" My answer is: "I'm not getting fed around here." Then, continuing my lament: "No one is feeding me." What do you think her response would be?

"Feed yourself!"[5]

There may be a place for spoon-feeding new believers at the beginning of their journey, but the ultimate goal is not to create spiritual dependency on another person. Instead, it is to help people learn how to feed themselves by creating a deep sense of dependency on the Holy Spirit. He is the master teacher, and he needs to be in control.

Will you listen to him and allow him to guide the process of making disciples? Will you allow him to speak and guide others to live in holiness? Will you trust him to convict, illuminate, and lead? Link discipleship to the Bible and then link the disciple to the Holy Spirit.

The process is simple. The curriculum is the Bible. The teacher is the Holy Spirit.

CONVICTION #4
THE **FOCUS** IS **OBEDIENCE**

Obedience-based discipleship.

Memorize that phrase, because it sits at the heart of the disciple-making process. The focus of our disciple-making activities is not the accumulation of biblical knowledge, the completion of a class, or the memorization of certain principles. The focus is always obedience. A disciple is an obedient follower of Jesus Christ, and in order to follow Jesus, a disciple needs to know how to hear from God.

In the first century, Jesus walked with his disciples, ate with them, gave them instructions, and modeled the perfect life. The early disciples knew whether they were following Jesus based on their intimate interaction with him as a physical person. Today, the situation is different. Jesus ascended to the Father. He is no longer with us in bodily form, and we can't look him in the eye to get verbal answers to our questions. Therefore, one of the necessary skills of a disciple of Christ is learning how to hear the voice of God. If we aren't regularly hearing from him, then we will not be able to follow or obey. God is always speaking. The question is whether we have learned how to listen. How do we hear from God? The answer is found in these short phrases:

The Word of God.

The Spirit of God.

The people of God.

These are the primary ways in which God speaks today. If people are growing in their hunger and knowledge of the Word of God, while regularly hearing from the Spirit of God and growing in community with the people of God, we are well on our way to making obedient disciples. These three phrases— the Word of God, the Spirit of God, the people of God—form the foundation for obedience-based group discipleship.

During every discipleship meeting, group members will uncover biblical knowledge, spiritual learning, and new insight. But the goal is not to learn Bible trivia. Instead, the mark of a true disciple is to be obedient to what they hear. Our goal as disciple makers is not to crank out Pharisees who can exegete Scripture, quote long sections of the Bible, or offer perfect theological answers for every situation.

Instead, we want to make disciples who obey. It's more application than information. Perhaps my favorite definition of discipleship is found in Eugene Peterson's writings: discipleship is a "long obedience in the same direction."[6] Paying close attention to the Word of God, the Spirit of God, and the people of God will allow us to move forward in obedience—and we must be disciplined to follow.

Discipulus is the Latin root word for both discipleship and discipline.[7] This definition reminds us that living a life of obedience is not always easy. But it is a requirement. You can't be a disciple of Christ and walk in disobedience to his commands. John Wesley once wrote that when a person hears from God, "whatever light you then receive, should be used to the uttermost, and that immediately. Let there be no delay. Whatever you resolve, begin to execute the first moment you can."[8] Furthermore, obedience and love ought to go hand in hand.

In fact, love is the Great Commandment summarizing all the Law and the Prophets (see Matt. 22:34–40). Obedient disciples are marked by love. Jesus shared this principle with his first disciples when he stated, "A new command I give you: Love one another. As I have loved you, so you must love one another. By this everyone will know that you are my disciples, if you love one another" (John 13:34–35).

Obedience and love.

At the end of the Gospel of John, a powerful story is shared about Jesus reinstating Peter after his denial of Christ. After the disciples had gone back to fishing, Jesus appeared and made them breakfast. When they had eaten, Jesus turned to the big fisherman and said, "Simon son of John, do you love me?" Simon said, "Yes, Lord, you know that I love you." Jesus said,

"Feed my lambs" (21:15). Three times Jesus tied the question of love to obedience. Perhaps Peter was reminded of Jesus' earlier statement in John 14:15, "If you love me, keep my commands."

The process is simple. The curriculum is the Bible. The teacher is the Holy Spirit. The focus is obedience.

CONVICTION #5
THE **RESULT** IS **MULTIPLICATION**

Let's recap for a moment.

Thus far, we have advocated for a simple, obedience-based model of group discipleship that is intimately linked to the Word of God, the Spirit of God, and the people of God. The goal of this model is to develop disciples that learn how to trust and obey Jesus in every aspect of their lives, and the result is multiplication.

The Bible tells us in Mark 1:17 that as Jesus was walking beside the Sea of Galilee, he saw Peter and his brother Andrew and called out to them, "Come, follow me." Do you remember the next words out of his mouth?

"Come, follow me, and we will study the Hebrew Scriptures together."

"Come, follow me, and we will do life together."

"Come, follow me, and learn the ways of the Master."

No. "Come, follow me," Jesus said, "and I will send you out to fish for people." The reason Jesus wanted Peter and Andrew to follow him, and the reason he calls us to live as his disciples, is that we might multiply our influence and fish for others. The fruit of making disciples ought to be multiplication. Discipleship is the primary engine for any type of multiplication movement.

Multiplication is close to the heart of God.

It was one of the first commands given to Adam and Eve in the Garden of Eden. "Be fruitful and multiply" (Gen. 1:22 ESV). Multiplication is a sign of God's blessing and creative work. Jesus ratified this theme of multiplication and blessing in the Gospels through his parables and miracles, and in the book of Acts, the Holy Spirit unleashes a multiplication movement for the early church. The language of reproduction is found throughout the whole Bible.

I am grateful for my current ministry assignment. I serve on an incredible team, and the lead pastor happens to be one of my best friends and shares my enthusiasm for making disciples. My position at the church is a bit unique, and during the hiring process, it was agreed that I could craft my own job description and title. I landed on the title "Multiplication Pastor".

It's not easy to explain that role to friends outside of the church. "What exactly does a multiplication pastor do?" they often ask. I regularly feel the need to inform them that my role has nothing to do with mathematics, multiplying fractions, or solving complex algorithms. It's not that kind of multiplication. Instead, my role is to help multiply disciples, leaders, and churches, in that order.

Disciple making comes first.

Jesus came to establish a disciple-making movement that would multiply throughout the world and find local expression in hundreds of thousands of churches around the globe. Some of those churches will meet in stadiums and others will meet in homes, but both ought to be expressions of discipleship that results in multiplication. Anything less and we fall short of God's design and calling for our lives.

In fact, if Jesus were to show up and evaluate our churches, his measuring stick of ministry effectiveness wouldn't be attendance, giving, professions of faith, baptisms, programming, or facilities. Instead, I'm convinced that one statistic would capture his attention above all the rest: number of disciples made. Those were his last words, and if we are doing it right, the result ought to be multiplication.

Let's review our framework for discipleship.

The process is simple. The curriculum is the Bible. The teacher is the Holy Spirit. The focus is obedience. The result is multiplication.

These five statements are the boundaries of the disciple-making playing field, and like Coach Lombardi's locker room talk, we need to stay focused on the fundamentals. But what happens next? How does a person disciple others? Is there a step-by-step process that we could implement? That will be our conversation in Part Two.

PART TWO

THE **PROCESS**

*A simple, step-by-step process for making
and multiplying disciples.*

Imagine the following scenario.

You are the pastor of a local church, and David has just crossed the line of faith. María has decided to surrender her life to Christ. Kasem is brand new to the church and spiritually hungry. Praise God! These people are ready to be discipled! So you approach a few people with a challenge. "Luis, will you disciple David? He's a new believer." "Katie, what would you think about discipling María and investing in her spiritually?" "Joel, Kasem is new to the church and needs to be discipled. I was thinking you might be able to help."

Luis, Katie, and Joel are more than willing. In fact, they are excited for the opportunity to disciple someone else. They're ready to jump in. But before they commit to this new adventure, they have one small problem. They don't know what to do! What does the disciple-making process actually look like?

This is where many books on discipleship fall silent or become incredibly confusing to follow. In order to be replicated, the discipleship process must be simple. In Part Two we will unpack an easy-to-follow, step-by-step guide for getting started in the adventure of making disciples. It is a process that will align with the framework from Part One.

STEP #1
SELECT **DISCIPLES**

It begins with selection.

In his book, *The Master Plan of Evangelism*, Robert Coleman names *selection* as the first and most important step in making disciples. Jesus' concern was never to develop programs to reach the multitudes, but to find men and women who the multitudes would follow. Before he ever preached a public sermon or impressed the crowds with a massive miracle, Jesus selected disciples.[1] Jesus realized that, although he loved everybody, he could only intentionally invest in twelve, and even then, his deepest influence would be made with three: Peter, James, and John.

Jesus did not take the process of selection lightly. Before choosing the twelve that would become his disciples, Jesus "went out to a mountainside to pray, and spent the night praying to God" (Luke 6:12). It's one of the few times in Scripture when we find Jesus investing an entire night in prayer.

Selecting the right disciples was a process Jesus took very seriously. He handpicked them.

We can learn a lot from his selection. Although he chose a diverse group of people from every walk of life, they had a few things in common. They were passionate about their work and committed to the task at hand. The disciples he chose were hungry to learn and teachable. They were also young. In fact, many scholars believe his disciples were ten to fifteen years younger than him, emphasizing the fact that Jesus understood the importance of investing in the next generation.[2] While others may have looked down their noses at the "unschooled, ordinary" individuals Jesus chose (see Acts 4:13), he understood their potential and desire to be used by God.

When selecting disciples, approach the process with focused prayer, and ask God to show you individuals with a desire to learn and grow. Jesus told his disciples in John 4:35, "I tell you, open your eyes and look at the fields! They are ripe for harvest." Prioritize those individuals who seem to be ripe for the harvest— the "good soil." Choose disciples who have a hunger for spiritual things. Life is too short to invest in working bad soil.[3]

It's now time to make a list.

Think about the connections God has given you, overlooking no one. Make a list of friends, neighbors, relatives, co-workers, and people at church who God might be leading you to disciple. Who are the people God has placed in your life? Which individuals seem most open to God and hungry for spiritual growth? Are there seekers or new believers who aren't in a discipleship relationship? When you finish your list, try to narrow it down to just three or four top candidates.

As a side note, if you have children, please consider starting a discipleship relationship with them as well. They are your highest priority.

Once you have a list of top candidates, it's time to make an invitation. The invitation should be presented as a high-level commitment. It will require sacrifice. It will require ongoing commitment. The participant will need to fully invest in the process, or it won't bear fruit. When you are recruiting disci- ples, set the bar high and issue the invitation as a challenge.

You could simply say, "I'm starting a discipleship group and I want to invite you to join me. Would you have time this week to get together and talk about it? I can walk you through the process and answer any questions you might have." Inviting the entire group of three or four people to the same orientation meeting can be beneficial.

STEP #2
START A DISCIPLESHIP GROUP

What is a discipleship group? A discipleship group is a gender-specific body of three to five people, meeting weekly for interactive Bible reading, accountability, and prayer for the lost. Let's unpack these characteristics one at a time.

Gender-Specific

John Wesley, an organizational genius and master at making disciples, established a simple structure of societies (large group gatherings), classes (small group gatherings), and bands (groups of three to five) to multiply the early Methodist movement. The smaller the setting, the higher the accountability.[4] All groups were mixed-gender except the band meetings. He kept band meetings gender-specific because of our human frailty, to avoid unneeded temptation, and to encourage more transparency.

Men and women are hardwired differently. While sin is universal, some struggles are gender-specific. For this reason, having gender-specific discipleship groups facilitates greater freedom in sharing and thus deeper understanding of one another.

There are inherent risks to openness and vulnerability in mixed-gender groups.[5] Husbands and wives may struggle to be sufficiently transparent. Plus, men and women in the group could develop inappropriate emotional connections. Certainly, there could be exceptions to this rule, but it is a good guideline to keep in mind. One day, in heaven, these gender issues will be behind us, but for now, the decision to be gender-specific is pragmatic and prudential.[6]

A Group of Three to Five People

Jesus almost always made disciples in groups. One could argue that Peter, James, and John were his original discipleship group. This doesn't preclude one-on-one discipleship and doesn't mean he never ministered to people individually, but the overall pattern in his ministry was group discipleship. There are several advantages to group discipleship, especially when it comes to multiplication.

Individual discipleship can create dependency on the leader and can easily morph into a counseling or therapy session.[7] One-on-one discipleship can also inhibit multiplication because of comparisons to the leader. My earlier illustration with Dr. Noll in Part One is a case in point. I could never be like him. Therefore, I never felt qualified to pursue my doctorate.

However, in a group environment, a person might be more open to multiplication, thinking, "I may never be like Maríka, but if Larry and Bubba can do this, maybe I can as well." Group discipleship also allows for more consistent meeting patterns, since a meeting doesn't necessarily need to be cancelled due to the absence of just one person. In some cases, it may make sense to begin a discipleship group with only two people, but we encourage groups to move toward three or four as quickly as possible and to never exceed five. Having more than five people in a group will often result in limited sharing and less accountability. Groups of three to five provide the best opportunities for meaningful interaction, consistency, and multiplication of disciples.

Meeting Weekly

Discipleship groups that meet every week are most effective. There is something sacred about the structure of gathering together every seven days for rest and restoration. Even if only two of your discipleship group members can meet, try to provide consistency as a leader. Determine a specific time and amount of time to meet each week and then commit to it. In our experience, most discipleship group meetings last sixty to ninety minutes, depending on the size of the group. The larger the group, the more time it may require. Most groups meet around kitchen tables, at coffee shops, or even in a back booth of a local restaurant. The key is consistency. The same is true if you are meeting virtually. Find a consistent time and place, and make the discipleship group meeting a lifelong discipline.

Now that you have selected your disciples and have a better understanding of the discipleship group, let's dive into the three primary practices of every discipleship group: interactive Bible reading, accountability, and prayer for the lost.

STEP #3

INTERACTIVE **BIBLE READING**

In our framework for discipleship in Part One, we emphasized the Bible as our core curriculum and encouraged every discipleship group member to follow a reading plan. After all, we plan our daily schedules, menus, exercise regimens, and weight loss plans. We plan our vacations, and some of us even plan the shows we watch.

We also need a plan to read the Bible.

In Appendix B, we've provided a plan for reading the New Testament, plus Psalms and Proverbs, in nine months. The summer months include a steady rotation of Old Testament books each year. This plan assumes that, every day, every disciple in your group will read at least one chapter of the Bible.

One chapter of the Bible. Every day.

But the reading needs to be interactive. I have often had the experience of reading a section of Scripture, putting my Bible down, and immediately forgetting most of what I read. I may not be the only one. With that in mind, we provide every discipleship group member a *Banding Together Journal*. This journal includes a discipleship group agenda, Bible reading plan, place for prayer requests, table of contents, and instructions on journaling. Journaling helps bring focus to our reading.

Every day, each disciple begins his or her reading of the Bible with prayer. Then, as they read, they seek to listen to the Holy Spirit.

They try to read slowly. Intentionally. Attentively.

Remember, the Holy Spirit is the teacher and will bring to light any words, phrases, or verses disciples need to hear. As the individual reads the chapter for the day, they underline anything that stands out to them. When they finish the chapter, they can either read it a second time or look back over what they've underlined and ask, "Lord, what do I need to hear from you today?"

The next step is to open a fresh page in their journal and record what they have heard the Spirit say. Here is a basic summary of the four-part journaling method we use, following a popular acronym called SOAP (Scripture, Observation, Application, Prayer).[8] Instructions for an alternate process are also explained in the opening pages of the *Banding Together Journal* and in Appendix C.

- First, write out a verse or passage of Scripture that the Holy Spirit has shown you for that day, as well as the reference.
- Second, look at the surrounding context of the verse you selected and write down anything important that you observe. Try to explain the passage in your own words.
- Third, ask how this verse might apply to your life. What is God calling you to do or to remember as a result? What is your next step, and how can you be obedient?
- Fourth, write out a closing prayer. This could be as short as a phrase or sentence, but use this final section to speak a request or commitment back to God.

One more thought on journaling. In our society, people often communicate their words through text messages or typed computer documents. Handwritten notes have gone by the wayside and become an almost ancient relic. We have lost the art of physical writing.

While technology can certainly be utilized in the process of journaling, there is something profound about putting thoughts on paper by hand. Encouraging letters from my parents and love notes from my wife that I've saved over the years have become sacred to me. Writing a physical journal entry slows down the process and allows more time to listen to the Spirit. It also eliminates needless distractions that often pop up when using computers, tablets, and smartphones. Only use technology for journaling as a last resort.

Interactive Bible reading is the foundation for our discipleship groups and will become the place for instruction through the Holy Spirit. He will convict, counsel, train, and guide. However, if obedience-based discipleship is our goal, we will need to learn the second practice of every discipleship group. It is the lost art of accountability.

STEP #4

ACCOUNTABILITY

"Fully known. Fully loved.[9]"

These four words represent the goal of accountability in every disciple-making relationship. In his book, *The Meaning of Marriage*, Timothy Keller summarized these statements by saying, "To be loved but not known is comforting but superficial. To be known and not loved is our greatest fear. But to be fully known and truly loved is, well, a lot like being loved by God."[10] God knows everything about us (fully known) and continues to love us unconditionally (fully loved).

We need individuals in our lives who are committed to doing the same. This requires creating an environment where people can be fully known, through confessing shortcomings, sins, hopes, and dreams, and at the same time fully loved, through regular displays of forgiveness, grace, and encouragement. While this can be the most difficult part of the discipleship process, it is required for a fruitful group. Let's look at each of these phrases one at a time.

Fully Known

Stop reading for a moment, and hold your breath for as long as you are able. How did you do? Most people can't hold their breath longer than sixty to ninety seconds. After that, the sensation that our lungs are bursting becomes too painful to endure. Where does that pain come from?

The oxygen we inhale is absorbed into our bloodstream and carried throughout the body. It is then converted to energy, which your body uses, and carbon dioxide, a waste product that it expels when you exhale. When you hold your breath, however, the carbon dioxide is trapped inside. If you don't exhale, you will eventually pass out. Interactive Bible reading is like inhaling the oxygen of the Word. Confession of sin is the process of exhaling after a long week.

Don't forget to exhale.

Being fully known involves being willing to confess your shortcomings to another person and to encourage one another to live in radical obedience to God. There must be a commitment to transparency and authenticity and a rejection of hypocrisy and secret living. The Bible promises in 1 John 1:9, "If we confess our sins . . . [God] will forgive us our sins." Praise God! However, forgiveness is only the first step in our healing. An alcoholic needs more than forgiveness. He also needs to be healed of his addiction.[11] God has promised us that confession of sin in biblical community will hasten our healing. James 5:16 states, "confess your sins to each other and pray for each other so that you may be healed."

God forgives our sin through repentance and sets up our healing through accountability and confession. His desire is to break "the power of canceled sin" as Charles Wesley once famously wrote.[12]

Fully Loved

Unfortunately, people are often hesitant to be transparent and fully known, primarily because of fear. The fear of rejection is strong. Therefore, the response to confession must be one of love and grace. When a confession is offered, it is important to bring encouragement and prayer, and always point people back to the gospel of Jesus Christ, reminding them not only of his forgiveness, but also the power he has given us through the Spirit. Put simply, confession should be answered with Christ-like love. This type of communal love for one another is the only way to grow in holiness. John Wesley famously wrote, "The gospel of Christ knows of no religion but social; no holiness but social holiness."[13] We need one another. Holiness is not a private, solitary thing to be achieved in isolation. Instead, it is learning to fully love one another despite our shortcomings.

Fully known. Fully loved. When these four words are lived out in a discipleship group, accountability will be most effective. To help spur this portion of the group, we have suggested ten accountability questions found in Appendix A and in the front cover of the *Banding Together Journal*. Many of these questions are taken from Wesley's band meetings, and others are designed to spur spiritual growth and increase love for God and one another.

Each day after doing the interactive Bible reading, individuals reflect on these daily accountability questions before God. Then, when the discipleship group meets each week, any shortcomings are confessed or victories celebrated. Rather than asking all ten questions during the group time, I often encourage group leaders to first allow members to share freely and then select only one or two questions they feel would be most important for their group to answer. Interactive Bible reading and accountability are the first two practices of any discipleship group. However, it is the third practice that keeps the groups moving outward.

Prayer for the lost.

PRAYER FOR THE **LOST**

Discipleship groups are not designed to be holy huddles.

If they devolve in that direction, they have lost their primary purpose. We gather to scatter. Our mission is to "go and make disciples," not "gather and make disciples." During the third and final practice of our discipleship groups, we spend time praying for those who are without Christ and look for opportunities to connect with them and share the good news of the gospel.

We pray for the lost.

Some people are uncomfortable with the word *lost* but it's perhaps the best word to describe those who are far from Christ. In the Gospel of Luke, Jesus told stories about a lost sheep and a lost coin. He concluded each by saying, "I tell you . . . there will be more rejoicing in heaven over one sinner who repents than over ninety-nine righteous persons who do not need to repent" (Luke 15:7). Jesus didn't come for the people who were already found. He came "to seek and to save the lost" (19:10).

Every parent can probably remember a time when they thought one of their children was lost. A few years ago, my wife was at the Chicago Aquarium with our four beautiful daughters when she realized that our three-year-old had wandered off. Each minute of searching felt like an hour. Security guards and other museum employees were notified, and after what seemed like days, she was finally located. I can tell you that in those moments, nothing was more important than finding her. The same should be true for those who are far from God. We must live with an urgency to pray for, serve, and seek out lost people. The next time you walk into a shopping mall, stadium event, coffee shop, or restaurant, ask yourself how many of those people are spiritually lost.

In our discipleship groups, we challenge group members to make a list of people they are praying would find their way back to God.[14] It might be a grocery store clerk, a waitress, a co-worker, or a neighbor. Perhaps the list includes family members, friends, or relatives. The important thing is that people in these groups are intentionally praying for the lost and finding ways to serve and connect with them.

We *must* disciple lost people into the kingdom. It is here that a few might want to separate evangelism and discipleship by saying that evangelism is for lost people and discipleship is for found people.

We don't make that distinction.

Instead, we see evangelism as the front end of disciple making and spiritual growth as the back end of the same process. Disciple making means helping people put their trust in Christ and then following him by living a life of obedience. Both are eternally and inextricably linked. Making disciples means relating to people far from God in such a way that they can come to faith in Christ and learn to follow him. Naturally, as they mature, they will be trained to repeat the process with others. Evangelism is simply a form of "pre-conversion discipleship."[15] Evangelism and discipleship are the front and back of the same coin.

Discipleship without prayer for the lost and multiplication is not genuine discipleship. Instead, it's a holy huddle. At the same time, evangelism without a healthy element of disciple making isn't evangelism. It is spiritual head hunting.[16] Neither of those options is acceptable. Biblical disciple making must include both.

Interactive Bible reading, accountability, and prayer for the lost are the three practices of every effective discipleship group. We will now close Part Two by walking through the entire process and the flow of a typical discipleship group meeting.

PUTTING IT ALL **TOGETHER**

THE DISCIPLESHIP GROUP EXPERIENCE

It's 8:00 on a Thursday night, and you are sitting at your local coffee shop waiting for your other discipleship group members to arrive. You have your Bible, journal, and pen and have just ordered a warm drink.

There was no lesson to prepare, no workbook that needed filled out, and no DVD or online curriculum to set up. Instead, your preparation for the meeting was your daily time reading the Bible, writing in your journal, reflecting on the accountability questions, listening to the Holy Spirit, and praying for those around you.

Soon your group members arrive, order coffee, and gather around. There are only four in your group, so everyone fits comfortably around one table in the back of the coffee shop. Your discipleship group spends a few minutes connecting about the events of the day. You transition by asking your group members about their weeks and then open with prayer.

After praying, you invite group members to open their Bibles and journals for the first part of the meeting.

Interactive Bible Reading

Because the curriculum is the Bible, and the teacher is the Holy Spirit, your primary role in the meeting is to facilitate, listen, and guide. You start with two opening questions that are listed in the discipleship group agenda on the inside cover of the *Banding Together Journal*:

- How many days did you read the Bible this week?
- Share from the Bible reading how you heard God speak and what he taught you.

The next thirty to sixty minutes are spent sharing how the Holy Spirit spoke to each of you through the daily Bible reading. Because group members participated in the guided journaling process, there is plenty to share, and each person is eager to tell how the Spirit has been speaking. Whenever someone shares their verse and journal entry, you all turn to that passage in your Bibles and offer your own insights and observations. You then move to the next person and continue until you sense it's time to switch gears. It's amazing to watch how the Holy Spirit guides the process, builds connections, and helps the group move forward. You also do your best as the group leader to listen attentively, correct any statements that are contrary to God's Word, and focus the conversation toward obedience. That's the goal.

End the interactive Bible reading with a third question: Did you have any questions from your reading? This allows the group leader to discern where the other disciples are in their spiritual journey and helps to flag any important questions individuals may need to wrestle through. If you don't know the answer to the questions, invite the group to do some research and come back the following week with any new insights. Then, if the interactive Bible reading doesn't naturally flow into accountability, encourage people to turn to their account-ability questions on the inside cover of the journals.

Accountability

Look at the ten accountability questions on the inside cover of the *Banding Together Journal* (and also in Appendix A) and begin your focus on accountability by asking group members if they have been obedient to all God has shown them this week. This is often the first and most important accountability question. Obedience-based discipleship means people must have a firm commitment to doing what God has told them to do.

Knowing the silence can be awkward at times, remind yourself not to rush forward. Wait a few seconds, quietly tapping your foot to the count of five. If nobody answers, you'll move on and pick one or two of the questions from the accountability list and invite people to answer. Perhaps there is something you need to share with the group as well. The key with this section is being honest and vulnerable as a leader and letting your group know it is a safe space. It is a process that requires trust, and trust takes time. Don't be discouraged if the group doesn't begin with complete transparency, but when a confession is made, encourage them and pray for them, always reminding them of the gospel.

Prayer for the Lost

The third part of your group meeting is prayer for the lost; invite group members to share names of people they are praying would come to Christ and updates on specific individuals. You remind group members to write the names of individuals they are praying for in the back few pages of the journal. You also invite group members to share their own specific prayer requests. Finally, close the group's time together in prayer for one another and the lost.

It's now been almost an hour to an hour and a half, and the group wraps up.

Between meetings, you'll check up on your discipleship group members, encouraging them in their struggles and possibly sharing your daily observations in God's Word. The most effective disciple making is developed in relationships, so consider spending time together outside of the group as well. When faithfully implemented over time, the discipleship group process ought to create an emerging picture of a disciple.

The Picture of a Disciple

I was scrolling through my TV playlist a while back and came across a hidden gem of a show that was produced in the late 1980s: *The Joy of Painting*, with Bob Ross. The show consists of thirty-minute episodes of a painter painting. I kid you not. That's it. It is literally watching paint dry.

I remember watching it with my grandpa when I was a little kid, and for old times' sake, I called my four children and wife together, and we watched an episode. For thirty minutes, Mr. Ross painted and then described his happy little trees, snow-capped mountains, and fluffy white clouds in his famously deep and hypnotic voice. It was a nostalgic moment, to be sure, and the kids were mesmerized as a beautiful picture of a landscape slowly emerged.

In less than a half hour, the blank canvas became a beautiful mountain scene, and at the end of the show, my seven-year-old daughter exclaimed, "Wait a minute, how did he do that?" It was a classic moment. It also reminded me of the emerging picture of a disciple.

The discipleship group process will take time.

The picture of an obedient disciple will not come into focus right away. The growth of the members in your discipleship group won't always be linear. There will be twists and turns along the way. Don't be discouraged. Over time, we are praying, a picture will emerge on the canvas. It will be the picture of a growing disciple.

What does that picture look like?

First, the growing disciple is learning to love God. They do this by reading the Bible every day, journaling any lessons learned, and faithfully walking in obedience to what the Spirit is saying. It is obedience-based discipleship. As Jesus said in John 14:15, "If you love me, keep my commands."

Second, the growing disciple is learning to love others. They are pursuing holiness by examining their lives and living in openness and transparency with others. They are confessing sin, becoming fully known, and extending God's grace to others in the group.

Finally, the growing disciple is learning what it means to love others beyond the group. They are praying for lost people, pursuing intentional relationships with others, and always looking for someone outside the discipleship group to pray for, serve, and perhaps lead to Christ. This is the picture of a disciple.

Loving God.

Loving one another.

Loving others.

Each disciple of Christ is a vital part of launching an even greater disciple-making movement. That will be our conversation in Part Three.

PART THREE

THE **MOVEMENT**

The right moves for unleashing a movement.

In the early 1990s, Peter Wagner was quoted as saying, "The single most effective evangelistic methodology under heaven is planting new churches."[1] I won't argue with his statement or the statistics that bear witness to his claim. Clearly, planting new churches is an effective evangelistic strategy, and people are attracted to new expressions of the kingdom. I only hope that in the process of planting new churches we don't forget our primary mission. Our primary mission is to make disciples.

My prayer is to see God birth a disciple-making, church-planting movement, and as I mentioned in the introduction, the order is incredibly important. Disciple making must be the priority.

That is the purpose behind writing this book. We need to reframe the conversation.

For too long, the conversation around multiplication has been waged at the macro level of church planting or church multiplication to the neglect of the micro level of disciples making disciples.[2] But I am convinced that disciple making is the only engine that will sustain a genuine movement of God.

When my family and I arrived in Dallas, Texas, almost a decade ago, I saw my role as that of a church planter. I felt called to plant a single church and be the founding pastor of a long, fruitful ministry. A few years later, God began to reveal to me that my calling was not to plant a single church but to plant multiple churches. So we moved to Des Moines, Iowa, to plant church number two and give ourselves to launching a church planting movement. I now realize that to accomplish that goal, we must have laser-like focus on intentional disciple making.

What will it take for you to not only make disciples but to also unleash a disciple-making movement in your church, campus, or community? What are the key moves you need to make? That is the focus of our next conversation.

MOVE #1

DISCOVER YOUR LEADERS

One of my favorite Bible stories revolves around a desperately poor widow and the prophet Elisha. The widow is experiencing a mountain of debt and can't seem to get out from under it. She feels overwhelmed.

Ever been there?

This overwhelming feeling is shared by many pastors, parents, and lay leaders regardless of the size of church or family or pace of life and ministry. Time, resources, and volunteers always seem to be in short supply, and people wonder how God will provide.

I love the way Elisha responds to the stressed widow. Elisha says, "Tell me, what do you have in your house?" The widow replies, "Your servant has nothing there at all . . . except a small jar of olive oil" (2 Kings 4:2). The story continues with the widow submitting the small jar of oil to the Lord, and a few verses later, we see the miracle of multiplication. In another story, Jesus preaches to thousands of hungry people. His disciples see no possible way to feed the masses, and they are overwhelmed by the hunger of the crowds. Jesus asks, "How many loaves do you have?" (Mark 6:38).

They only had five loaves and two fish, but that was all that was needed for the miracle of multiplication. Similar conversations have taken place with Abraham, Moses, David, and thousands of other men and women throughout the ages. God takes what we have and multiplies it. If you feel overwhelmed at the prospect of launching a disciple-making movement in your church or community, I have a simple question to ask.

Who do you have?

Many of the great disciple-making movements of history began with only a few committed people who were fully surrendered to God. The widow responded, "your servant has nothing there at all . . . except a small jar of olive oil" (2 Kings 4:2). You may say, "I have no one here at all—except Jamal." Praise God for Jamal! The Lord is going to use both of you to launch a disciple-making movement in your church or neighborhood. God doesn't need much.

Discover your leaders.

The key with this first move is to determine which people in your sphere of influence could be characterized as obedient disciples of Christ. They don't need to be highly educated or lifelong veterans of the faith. They simply need to be fully surrendered to Jesus. These are the individuals God will use to start a disciple-making movement in your church or community.

Also, try to identify an equal number of men and women. Since discipleship groups are gender-specific, it's good to have both genders equally represented. Make a list. Whether you are in a neighborhood moms' group, serving in a new church plant, or pastoring a large, established church of thousands, God has given you a select group of people to get started.

Earlier in this book, we talked about selecting *disciples*. I'm now asking you to select *disciple makers*. The same principles apply, only now we are looking for a higher degree of spiritual maturity. If you aren't sure where to start, you may want to consult a few trusted friends or colleagues to build this growing list of obedient disciples.

Don't overlook anyone. Some of the greatest disciple-making movements around the world, in countries like India and China, are happening through teenage girls, marginalized people groups, and those who have been consistently overlooked.

Pray. Fast. Listen to the Holy Spirit.

The next step is to invite those on your list to the first gathering of disciple makers. Remember, this isn't simply another program of the church. You are praying for a movement, and it will begin with the people you have invited into the room. They are the ones who will carry it forward.

At this gathering, cast the vision for making disciples and launching a disciple-making movement through discipleship groups. Be sure to engage this gathering with a heart full of passion and vision for fulfilling the final words of Christ to "go and make disciples." You may want to give people a copy of this book to read before the meeting and a *Banding Together Journal* to help them learn the processes. When you have finished sharing, give them a week or two to respond to your challenge.

The next step is training.

MOVE #2
MODEL THE PROCESS

I'll never forget that morning.

Leading up to that Sunday, I had invested hours in preparing a sermon that would be faithful, relevant, engaging, entertaining, and passionate. During that season of ministry, our church plant felt a bit fragile, and there was no room for anything less than a dynamic and spiritually charged message. I was preaching what I believed to be a rousing sermon, when suddenly and almost unexpectedly, I stopped. It had dawned on me, as I was wrapping up the most powerful point in my message, that most people in the congregation seemed uninspired. What I saw looking back at me were empty stares. A young lady in the back yawned. An older gentleman checked his watch.

I abruptly ended the sermon.

Something inside of me wanted to cry out, "Why exactly are you even here?" Fortunately, I didn't go with that impulse but instead invited our worship team to come forward and closed out the morning with an extended time of worship. I left the building that morning with a lot of bottled-up frustration.

A few months later, I came across a statement that expressed my emotions that day. The author wrote, "We need to spend less time and effort figuring out how to get cultural Christians to stay and more time and energy making disciples who will *go!*"[3] Yes, that was it. That was the answer to the frustration I was feeling.

That statement was a paradigm shift in my understanding of the purpose of the church. Rather than thinking of my congregation as a place that provided religious goods and services on the weekend, I needed to think of them as a training center for future disciple makers. If your context isn't a local church, perhaps that training center is your house or a meeting hall or public gathering. The essence of this move is the importance of mobilization, and if your first move was successful, you ought to have a few individuals who are ready to join you on this journey. It's now time for training.

It's time to model the process.

Training can typically last for six weeks with the content of the training being an explanation of the five-part framework of Part One and modeling the five-part process of Part Two. Explaining and modeling. Break your leaders down into gender-specific groups of three to four people and model the discipleship group process.

When my church first launched our disciple-making movement, we had twenty-four leaders respond to the call to make disciples. This required me to meet with six different groups of four people every week for six weeks. It was a ten-hour commitment on my part to lead the groups each week, but it was the only way for people to experience a discipleship group as part of the modeling process.

Churches that are larger may need to add another layer of training to accommodate the process. Churches that are smaller or individuals who are launching a disciple-making movement in their communities may begin with only one or two groups of disciple makers. Whatever the context, model the disciple-making process well for your future leaders.

Remember, there is nothing more important than making disciples. In fact, this new shift in thinking will require you to prioritize more and more of your time, energy, and effort around training and equipping disciple makers. John Wesley stressed the use of lay leaders in the ministries of the church by both precept and example. He taught that the primary function of spiritual and educational leadership was to equip others to lead and minister, not to perform the ministry personally.[4]

The typical mind-set of many pastors and church leaders is, "We can do it, you can help." However, when we begin to see our churches as places to mobilize disciple makers rather than places to gather believers, there will be a shift in the collective mind-set that is better expressed by the phrase, "You can do it; we can help."[5]

This training can be delivered by simply modeling the discipleship group process with your future disciple makers. Begin the reading plan, start the journaling, ask accountability questions, and begin praying for the lost. Remember, the goal at the end of the six weeks is for each person in the training to begin his or her own group.

That brings us to our third move.

MOVE #3
LAUNCH THE MOVEMENT

God has given you some incredible men and women to start this movement, and they are now trained and ready to go. During the final training session, commission your disciple makers to start the process outlined in Part Two. You may have a few people who don't feel ready to launch, in which case you can have them join another group.

It's now time to hit the ignition button and release each one to recruit three others and start meeting in their own discipleship groups. Congratulations! You have established the basic building blocks and DNA of disciple making in your church or community, and the number of individuals in your disciple-making ministry just multiplied by three. Here are a few things to remember.

This Is Not a Program

Disciple making is a lifestyle, not a program. Don't forget, "You can do it; we can help." Moving forward, your role is to assist others as they make disciples. People who want to branch out and start new groups must listen to the Holy Spirit and be obedient. Your job is to help in whatever way you can. Don't hold them back!

Certainly, it would be wise to offer ongoing discipleship training and a process to engage the spiritual formation of your leaders, but please resist the temptation to control this movement of God. We would never stand in the way of a group of people in the church wanting to gather for prayer. We would never argue with people wanting to share their faith. Why, then, do we often try to control disciple-making activities? Perhaps because we have failed to recognize that the Holy Spirit is the teacher.

First John 2:27 tells us, "As for you, the anointing you received from him remains in you, and you do not need anyone to teach you. But as his anointing teaches you about all things and as that anointing is real, not counterfeit . . . remain in him." We want to see more and more people engaged in a disciple-making lifestyle and we must resist the urge to treat this as a program of the church but instead encourage people to remain in him.

This Is Not a Promotion

Notice that nothing has been said about promoting this ministry through the website, through weekend worship services, or through the announcements of the church. Instead, the launch of the movement happens through existing relationships, and most of it takes place underground and off the radar. Launching the movement should not be done with fanfare, bumper videos, or some type of public celebration. Rather, I would encourage you to create a groundswell of intentional, relational discipleship through existing networks. Yes, eventually the ministry will get so large that simple systems will need to be put in place to keep it moving, but not at first. During the launch phase of the movement, simply release your leaders and allow it to build organically.

This Is Not a Sprint

Think long term and persevere. This disciple-making movement will take time, but eventually it will gain some serious momentum. Jesus compared the kingdom of heaven to a mustard seed, saying, "Though it is the smallest of all seeds, yet when it grows, it is the largest of garden plants and becomes a tree" (Matt. 13:31–32). If we give the mustard seed of disciple making enough time, it will multiply beyond our expectations. The shortcut method of church growth without disciple making will never produce a sustained movement.

Nineteenth century theologian Augustus Strong told of a student who asked the president of Oberlin College if he could take a shorter course than the one prescribed. "Oh yes", the president replied, "but then it depends on what you want to make of yourself. When God wants to make an oak, He takes a hundred years, but when He wants to make a squash, He takes six months."[6]

Launching a disciple-making movement will not happen overnight. This is not a sprint and it will have its challenges. John Wesley understood this well. He once remarked, "But the bands (small groups of 3-5) in every place need continual instruction. For they are continually flying to pieces."[7] However, with perseverance and oversight, the movement we are praying for will begin to take root in the church and community as people begin to be changed by the consistent repetition of interactive Bible reading, accountability, and prayer for the lost.

Now that the first wave of discipleship groups has launched, there is another critical move to make as we continue to push the movement forward.

MOVE #4

GATHER FOR QUARTERLY MEETINGS

By this point in the process, discipleship groups are actively meeting across the community. They meet in coffee shops, homes, church classrooms, restaurants, athletic clubs, office buildings, fitness centers, and anywhere else that three to five people can gather. It is easy to feel excited when you are leading the overall movement, but each individual group can start to feel isolated or alone in making disciples.

Enter the quarterly meeting.

The quarterly meeting is a regular meeting pattern of gathering all the discipleship group leaders and group members together four times a year. This type of meeting is not without precedent.

In the early Wesleyan system, the pastors and lay leaders in a specific area would meet quarterly to share in worship, testimonies, and the business of the church. These quarterly meetings became especially encouraging to the smaller congregations and communities flung out across the frontier or countryside. Gathering together in a larger setting allowed people to witness the growing strength of the movement and even participate in shaping its future direction. Furthermore, in early American Methodism, these meetings morphed into camp meetings and revivals.[8] They became pivotal moments in pushing the movement forward.

These gatherings are crucial to building momentum.

In my church's context, we hold quarterly meetings on Sunday evenings. These gatherings include worship, training in disciple making, testimonies, and often communion. They are inspirational, filled with vision and praise, and always end with a call to continue to press forward in making and multiplying disciples. If you are launching a movement outside of the church, perhaps you could rent a park shelter, find a community center, or host a quarterly meeting in your home.

Initially, we used the quarterly gatherings exclusively for our existing discipleship group leaders and participants. However, we have now promoted our quarterly meetings publicly to allow others the opportunity to learn more about discipleship groups and disciple making. The quarterly meeting is now an on-ramp to the growing movement and a place to integrate new disciple makers and participants.

If you are launching a disciple-making movement outside of the church, I could envision these quarterly meetings as the seeds of a future expression of the church or even the beginning of a new church plant. Perhaps God is using you to establish a new church and you didn't even know it! Please invest in these gatherings. Spiritually. Relationally. Financially.

In most churches today, the bulk of the ministry budget is invested in weekend worship services that include children's and students' programming, technology, and production. This sends a clear signal that the church is all about the weekend. What would it look like to align a larger portion of your resources around this disciple-making movement?

Perhaps you could resource group leaders with top-notch training and group members with free journals or study Bibles. This reallocation of funds will be crucial in keeping energy behind the movement.

Finally, make these quarterly meetings count. If you are in an established church, be sure to leverage the quarterly meeting as one of the most important gatherings of the year, the place where a disciple-making movement is forming. Be sure to give it your best attention and greatest effort. Spend consistent time in prayer for these gatherings and ask the Holy Spirit to reveal himself in a mighty way.

Let's recap our first four moves in the form of four questions:

Who do you have?
How will you train them?
How will you release them?
How will you gather them back together?

It's time for move number five.

MOVE #5

IMPLEMENT **SIMPLE** SYSTEMS

One of the greatest disciple makers ever to live was John Wesley. He understood that without discipline and structure, most new converts would drift back to their old ways of worldly living. Simple systems were crucial to the growth of the movement and the latticework on which the vine would flourish.

Wesley's genius, and the reason the Methodist movement survived, was his blueprint for discipleship. The societies, classes, and bands that he started became the operating system, and the simple structure supported the expanding movement.

This brings us to the fifth and final move.

When the church wakes up to the mission of Jesus and a disciple-making movement begins, there are a few simple systems that should to be considered. You should begin to think about on-ramps for finding new disciples, ongoing training for disciple makers, quarterly gatherings for sustaining momentum, and communications and resourcing. These four systems don't need to be complicated, but they do need to be implemented. Let's take each system one at a time for consideration in your context.

Integration System

The most effective way to bring new disciples into the movement is through personal invitation. Disciple making works best when it happens organically through existing relationships. However, when existing relational networks are exhausted, or when God pours out his favor and dozens of people put their trust in Christ and are baptized, how will you bring them into discipleship groups? How will you integrate new people into your disciple-making ministry?

Training System

Ongoing training of discipleship group leaders is crucial to the success of the movement. We currently use a six-week training process that I briefly touched on to get people out of the starting gate and into disciple making. However, beyond the initial training, it will be important to provide ongoing, regular training for discipleship group leaders. These ongoing training events could be done online, one-on-one, in classrooms, or in any other venue you see fit. The important thing is to regularly bring leaders together to debrief and train in a new disciple-making skill. How will you provide ongoing training for discipleship group leaders?

Quarterly Meeting System

We spent time explaining the philosophy behind the quarterly meeting event, but it will be wise to have someone leading the coordinating and planning process. I imagine your church has some type of worship planning system, and I encourage you to leverage those teams in planning these events. If you are launching a movement outside of the church, consider bringing in outside help for support. Because this is the largest gathering of the movement, think through the order of service, agenda, and outcomes you are hoping to achieve. How will you coordinate the quarterly meeting gatherings?

Communication System

Depending on the size of your initial group of disciple makers, most communication can be done through personal conversation or email. However, as the movement grows, you will need to consider the best format for sharing information on dates, trainings, quarterly meetings, and resourcing. Where can people pick up journals and Bibles? When is the next quarterly meeting and where? Are there online resources you want them to consider? Do you want to provide online surveys for feedback? Are there notes of encouragement you want to provide? What will be your system for communication and resourcing discipleship group leaders and members?

The tension in any movement is to provide enough structure to sustain the movement while at the same time enough flexibility to continue to adapt.[9] Finding this balance is not always easy and will require much prayer and discernment. However, these four simple systems will provide the necessary backbone.

PUTTING IT ALL **TOGETHER**

THE DISCIPLESHIP GROUP MOVEMENT

You have finally decided to take the plunge!

Rather than limiting your influence with a few individuals in your discipleship group, you have decided to go all in and launch a disciple-making movement.

Perhaps you are leading this movement in your neighborhood, on your college campus, through a sports team, or even at work. However, since many people reading this book serve in a local church, let's use that context to illustrate how this movement might unfold.

Imagine you are currently leading a stable ministry of seventy-five to eighty people in average worship attendance and are committed to building a disciple-making movement in your church and community. This simple guide has inspired you to take the first step.

You begin by compiling a list of individuals who you would consider obedient disciples. There are several "old saints" who come to mind, as well as a handful of younger couples with kids and a few empty nesters. You share the list with a few trusted board members and friends and end up with ten names of people to recruit. You personally call each of them and invite them to a gathering where you will share more about the vision God has given you for launching a disciple-making movement.

A week before the meeting, you enlist a few prayer warriors to intercede on your behalf and ask God to give you the right words to say and the passion to say them well. On the night of the meeting, God comes through, and your message resonates with each one. It's hard for anyone to argue with a clear focus on disciple making and a compelling vision. You ask people to spend a week in prayer, and nine out of ten of the individuals make the commitment to go through the training.

Move #1 is complete.

Immediately, you put a date on the calendar for your first week of training and divide your future disciple makers into two groups according to gender. Four men and five women are in two separate groups. You use the six-week training process to model what a discipleship group looks like, and during the final session of the training, you encourage each of your future group leaders to make a list of people they would like to invite into their new discipleship groups. You close the final session by spending extra time in prayer. One person informs you after the meeting that they have decided they aren't ready to lead a group and would rather partner up with someone else. No worries!

Move #2 is complete.

You now have eight groups ready to form.

It's time to release them to "go and make disciples." You stay in communication with each one until their groups form, and you are surprised by their excitement at finally having a clear process to follow when it comes to making disciples.

All eight do a fantastic job of recruiting, and a few of the groups have even brought in individuals from outside the church. You now have thirty-two adults involved in discipleship groups, and you are already beginning to see how this process could spill over to students and children. The eight groups are now meeting around town in coffee shops and restaurants, and frequently, you pop into the local diner and see a group gathered around the table. Praise God!

Move #3 is complete.

You have been starting to think through the necessary systems to sustain this movement, and you enlist your worship director to help plan the first quarterly gathering. You send the invitation to each of the discipleship group leaders, and the first quarterly meeting is a huge success.

Thirty of your discipleship group members show up, and ten more from the church and community are also in attendance. Looking out at the forty people assembled, you develop a sense of resolve when it comes to disciple making. This will be the new direction for your church in the future.

Move #4 is complete.

One year later, three of the groups have multiplied, bringing the total number of discipleship groups to eleven, and now over half of your congregation and a large majority of the adults are involved in a weekly discipleship relationship. Word is beginning to travel in the church, and there is growing conversation about what can only be described as an underground disciple-making movement.

It won't be long until the movement impacts the entire church and begins to spill over into the community. In fact, one of your discipleship groups is made up of four college students who have shared a growing burden to start making disciples on their campus. Who knows? Perhaps a new church will form out of their ministry. The possibilities are endless.

Fortunately, you have put simple systems in place to sustain whatever the Holy Spirit wants to do. You don't want to see this movement fade. You are hoping this is just the beginning.

Move #5 is complete.

By God's grace, you took the introduction of this book to heart, studied and followed the framework listed in Part One, implemented the simple disciple-making process of Part Two, and courageously started a broader discipleship movement by following the moves of Part Three. Indeed, the best days are yet to come!

CONCLUSION
BANDING TOGETHER

The band meeting was a key aspect of John Wesley's strategy for disciple making. These small groups of three to five people were an integral part of sustaining the greater movement of God in the 18th and early 19th centuries. The primary emphasis of each meeting was the confession of sin, and while Wesley had a specific purpose for itinerant field preaching, societies, and classes, it was the band meeting where the deepest level of discipleship took place.

In 1798, after the Methodist movement crossed the Atlantic and began to spread across America, Francis Asbury wrote, ". . . where these meetings of the bands have been kept up in their life and power, the revival of the work of God has been manifest both in the addition of members to the society, and in the deepening of the life of God in general."[1] We can't overestimate the impact of band meetings as they formed both the undergirding and fuel for the greater movement. This idea of banding together in group discipleship formed a core part of the disciple-making strategy of the Wesleyan movement. It is also a core element of the strategy advocated in this book.

Discipleship groups are designed to function like early band meetings, but with a greater emphasis on interactive Bible reading and prayer for the lost. We live in a biblically illiterate society and have lost a baseline understanding of the Word of God. It is our conviction that accountability must begin with obedience to God's Word. Banding together means coming around a core set of convictions and practices to move forward in holiness and the mission of the church. While account-ability and confession of sin are integral to each discipleship group, the practices of daily Bible reading and prayer for the lost provide the oxygen for moving groups forward. I suppose you could say we band together in discipleship groups to pre-pare for the greater movement God has in store. We gather to scatter and the mission of disciple making must always be front and center.

The Mission

Making disciples is the primary mission God has given every follower of Christ and every church. The Bible speaks of the church as a place of worship, fellowship, evangelism, teach-ing, ministry, prayer, service, and a host of other activities. But each of these purposes of the church ultimately falls under the priority of disciple making. That is the Great Commission. In our local church, we have decided to adopt a very simple mission statement: "Making disciples who make disciples."[2]

C.S. Lewis writes in his book, *Mere Christianity*, "The Church exists for nothing else but to draw men into Christ, to make them little Christs. If they are not doing that, all the cathedrals, clergy, missions, sermons, even the Bible itself, are simply a waste of time."[3] Another modern saint of the church, Dietrich Bonhoeffer, wrote in his landmark book, *The Cost of Discipleship*, "Christianity without discipleship is always Christianity without Christ."[4]

The church exists to make women and men more like Jesus. Our role as followers of Christ is to help others place their trust in Jesus and follow him as his disciples. Which begs the question: if we aren't making disciples, what exactly are we doing?

Making and multiplying disciples ought to be the primary thing. It ought to be the topic of conversation, the focus of planning meetings, the subject of celebration, and the metric of measurement. Churches and people measure all sorts of things that aren't the main thing: attendance in weekend worship, per capita giving, number of students in the youth ministry, missionary giving, membership, and the list goes on. These are important, but the greater question for churches ought to be, "How many disciples have you made in the last year?" And the question we should be asking one another is even more specific.

Who are you discipling?

There has been a lot of debate over the years when it comes to models of ministry. People debate whether the church should be more attractional, missional, traditional, contemporary, modern, house-based, ancient-future, liturgical, community-driven, and so on. I'm not sure if those debates are as important as answering a simple question:

How can we make more and better disciples? That is our mission.

One of the books that sits prominently on my shelf is David Garrison's *Church Planting Movements*.[5] In the pages of the book, he chronicles a few of the incredible movements of God taking place around the world. I first read the book almost a decade ago and recently picked it up again to refresh myself with the material. After a second reading, I was reminded that he could have easily titled the book, *Disciple-Making Movements*. In fact, there wasn't a single church-planting movement where disciple making wasn't the primary focus. God's power is being poured out around the world wherever there is an intense focus on banding together and making disciples.

A Final Word

This guide was written in a practical, pragmatic, and straight-forward manner with necessary convictions, steps, and moves. We've called it a practical guide for disciple makers. I'm sure it's imperfect, and maybe you will find ways to build upon this foundation and do an even better job of making and multiplying disciples. But if you read this book and only come away inspired, the purpose of this book has not been fulfilled.

You must move beyond the inspiration of ideas. You must stop talking about discipleship in vague generalities that don't lead to action. It's time to move. It's time to act. It's time to make disciples. When people talk about good intentions with no plan for executing them, I'm reminded of a quote by Peter Drucker, the father of modern management. He writes that many brilliant people falsely believe that ideas move mountains. Then he continues, "But bulldozers move mountains; ideas show where the bulldozers should go to work."[6]

Let's remind ourselves of our marching orders and get to work. Jesus chose to spend his life making disciples, and for the bulk of his three-and-a-half-year ministry on earth, he modeled disciple making. He then commanded his followers to do the same. When he completed his work Jesus told his disciples, "As the Father has sent me, I am sending you" (John 20:21). He then gathered them together before ascending to the Father, uttering these famous words, "All authority in heaven and on earth has been given to me. Therefore go and make disciples of all nations, baptizing them in the name of the Father and of the Son and of the Holy Spirit, and teaching them to obey everything I have commanded you. And surely I am with you always, to the very end of the age" (Matt. 28:18–20).

The final words of Christ aren't called the Great Suggestion or the Great Opinion or the Great Idea for the church. They are appropriately titled the Great Commission. A *commission* is "an instruction, command, or role given to a person or group of people."[7] You have been given an incredibly significant command. God has called you to be a disciple maker.

I wonder what would happen if each one of us made a concerted effort through prayer and hard work to diligently and obediently press into the Great Commission and focus on making disciples.

The result might be a movement.

For additional coaching and training in the area of discipleship or to learn more about implementing discipleship groups in your church or community, please visit www.bandingtogether.net.

APPENDIX A
SAMPLE **DISCIPLESHIP GROUP** AGENDA

Bible Reading

1. How many days did you read the Bible this week?
2. How did you hear God speak this week? Share a journal entry.
3. Did you have any questions from your reading?

Accountability

1. In what areas are you experiencing victory over sin?
2. What known sins have you committed since our last meeting?
3. What temptations have you encountered and how were you delivered?
4. What have you thought, said, or done and wondered if it was sin?
5. How has the Holy Spirit been testing and growing you this week?
6. Have you been angry, fearful, or anxious this week? Why?

7. How have you battled sexual temptation or struggled with intimacy and how are you preparing to deal with it?

8. Do you need to reconcile with anyone? Are you holding a grudge or envious of another?

9. Who can you show greater love to in the week to come? How will you do it?

10. Are there any other questions you would like to have asked each week?

Prayer for Lost

1. Who were you able to connect with or serve outside of the church this week?

2. Who are you praying would surrender their life to Christ?

3. Who is someone you could potentially disciple in the future?

Close in prayer for the lost and one another.

APPENDIX B

YEARLY **READING PLAN**

By following this plan, you will read through the New Testament, Psalms, and Proverbs once a year. In the summer, choose one of the provided options from the Old Testament to complete that reading every four years.

JANUARY

1 ☐ Luke 1
2 ☐ Luke 2
3 ☐ Luke 3; Ps. 1
4 ☐ Luke 4
5 ☐ Luke 5; Ps. 2
6 ☐ Luke 6
7 ☐ Luke 7
8 ☐ Luke 8
9 ☐ Luke 9
10 ☐ Luke 10
11 ☐ Luke 11
12 ☐ Luke 12
13 ☐ Luke 13; Ps. 3
14 ☐ Luke 14; Ps. 4
15 ☐ Luke 15; Ps. 5
16 ☐ Luke 16; Ps. 6
17 ☐ Luke 17; Ps. 7
18 ☐ Luke 18
19 ☐ Luke 19
20 ☐ Luke 20
21 ☐ Luke 21; Ps. 8
22 ☐ Luke 22
23 ☐ Luke 23
24 ☐ Luke 24
25 ☐ Acts 1; Ps. 9
26 ☐ Acts 2
27 ☐ Acts 3; Ps. 10
28 ☐ Acts 4; Ps. 11
29 ☐ Acts 5
30 ☐ Acts 6; Ps. 12
31 ☐ Review

FEBRUARY

1 ☐ Acts 7; Ps. 13
2 ☐ Acts 8
3 ☐ Acts 9
4 ☐ Acts 10
5 ☐ Acts 11; Ps. 14
6 ☐ Acts 12; Ps. 15
7 ☐ Acts 13
8 ☐ Acts 14; Ps. 16
9 ☐ Acts 15
10 ☐ Acts 16
11 ☐ Acts 17; Ps. 17
12 ☐ Acts 18; Ps. 18:1–19
13 ☐ Acts 19; Ps. 18:20–50
14 ☐ Acts 20; Ps. 19
15 ☐ Acts 21
16 ☐ Acts 22; Ps. 20
17 ☐ Acts 23; Ps. 21
18 ☐ Acts 24; Ps. 22:1–18
19 ☐ Acts 25; Ps. 22:19–31
20 ☐ Acts 26; Ps. 23
21 ☐ Acts 27; Ps. 24
22 ☐ Acts 28; Ps. 25
23 ☐ Gal. 1; Ps. 26
24 ☐ Gal. 2; Ps. 27
25 ☐ Gal. 3; Ps. 28
26 ☐ Gal. 4; Ps. 29
27 ☐ Gal. 5; Ps. 30
28 ☐ Review
29 ☐ Review

MARCH
1 ☐ Gal. 6; Ps. 31
2 ☐ 1 Cor. 1; Ps. 32
3 ☐ 1 Cor. 2; Ps. 33
4 ☐ 1 Cor. 3; Ps. 34
5 ☐ 1 Cor. 4; Ps. 35
6 ☐ 1 Cor. 5; Ps. 36
7 ☐ 1 Cor. 6; Ps. 37:1–22
8 ☐ 1 Cor. 7
9 ☐ 1 Cor. 8; Ps. 37:23–40
10 ☐ 1 Cor. 9; Ps. 38
11 ☐ 1 Cor. 10; Ps. 39
12 ☐ 1 Cor. 11; Ps. 40
13 ☐ 1 Cor. 12; Ps. 41
14 ☐ 1 Cor. 13; Ps. 42
15 ☐ 1 Cor. 14
16 ☐ 1 Cor. 15
17 ☐ 1 Cor. 16; Ps. 43
18 ☐ 2 Cor. 1; Ps. 44
19 ☐ 2 Cor. 2; Ps. 45
20 ☐ 2 Cor. 3; Ps. 46
21 ☐ 2 Cor. 4; Ps. 47
22 ☐ 2 Cor. 5; Ps. 48
23 ☐ 2 Cor. 6; Ps. 49
24 ☐ 2 Cor. 7; Ps. 50
25 ☐ 2 Cor. 8; Ps. 51
26 ☐ 2 Cor. 9; Ps. 52
27 ☐ 2 Cor. 10; Ps. 53
28 ☐ 2 Cor. 11; Ps. 54
29 ☐ 2 Cor. 12; Ps. 55
30 ☐ 2 Cor. 13
31 ☐ Review

APRIL
1 ☐ Mark 1; Ps. 56
2 ☐ Mark 2; Ps. 57
3 ☐ Mark 3; Ps. 58
4 ☐ Mark 4–5
5 ☐ Mark 6; Ps. 59
6 ☐ Mark 7; Ps. 60
7 ☐ Mark 8; Ps. 61
8 ☐ Mark 9
9 ☐ Mark 10; Ps. 62
10 ☐ Mark 11; Ps. 63
11 ☐ Mark 12
12 ☐ Mark 13; Ps. 64
13 ☐ Mark 14; Ps. 65
14 ☐ Mark 15
15 ☐ Mark 16; Ps. 66
16 ☐ 1 Thess. 1; Ps. 67
17 ☐ 1 Thess. 2; Ps. 68:1–18
18 ☐ 1 Thess. 3; Ps. 68:19–35
19 ☐ 1 Thess. 4; Ps. 69:1–16
20 ☐ 1 Thess. 5; Ps. 69:17–36
21 ☐ 2 Thess. 1; Ps. 70
22 ☐ 2 Thess. 2; Ps. 71
23 ☐ 2 Thess. 3; Ps. 72

24 ☐ Rom. 1; Ps. 73:1–15
25 ☐ Rom. 2; Ps. 73:16–28
26 ☐ Rom. 3; Ps. 74
27 ☐ Rom. 4; Ps. 75
28 ☐ Rom. 5; Ps. 76
29 ☐ Rom. 6; Ps. 77
30 ☐ Review

MAY
1 ☐ Rom. 7; Ps. 78:1–20
2 ☐ Rom. 8; Ps. 78:21–55
3 ☐ Rom. 9; Ps. 78:56–72
4 ☐ Rom. 10; Ps. 79
5 ☐ Rom. 11; Ps. 80
6 ☐ Rom. 12; Ps. 81
7 ☐ Rom. 13; Ps. 82
8 ☐ Rom. 14; Ps. 83
9 ☐ Rom. 15; Ps. 84
10 ☐ Rom. 16; Ps. 85
11 ☐ Eph. 1; Ps. 86
12 ☐ Eph. 2; Ps. 87
13 ☐ Eph. 3; Ps. 88
14 ☐ Eph. 4; Ps. 89:1–18
15 ☐ Eph. 5; Ps. 89:19–35
16 ☐ Eph. 6; Ps. 89:36–52
17 ☐ Phil. 1; Ps. 90
18 ☐ Phil. 2; Ps. 91
19 ☐ Phil. 3; Ps. 92
20 ☐ Phil. 4; Ps. 93
21 ☐ Col. 1; Ps. 94
22 ☐ Col. 2; Ps. 95
23 ☐ Col. 3; Ps. 96
24 ☐ Col. 4; Ps. 97
25 ☐ 1 Tim. 1; Ps. 98
26 ☐ 1 Tim. 2; Ps. 99
27 ☐ 1 Tim. 3; Ps. 100
28 ☐ 1 Tim. 4; Ps. 101
29 ☐ 1 Tim. 5; Ps. 102
30 ☐ 1 Tim. 6; Ps. 103
31 ☐ Review

SEPTEMBER
1 ☐ Matt. 1; Ps. 104:1–18
2 ☐ Matt. 2; Ps. 104:19–35
3 ☐ Matt. 3; Ps. 105:1–22
4 ☐ Matt. 4; Ps. 105:23–45
5 ☐ Matt. 5
6 ☐ Matt. 6; Ps. 106:1–12
7 ☐ Matt. 7; Ps. 106:13–48
8 ☐ Matt. 8; Ps. 107:1–22
9 ☐ Matt. 9; Ps. 107:23–43
10 ☐ Matt. 10
11 ☐ Matt. 11; Ps. 108
12 ☐ Matt. 12
13 ☐ Matt. 13
14 ☐ Matt. 14; Ps. 109:1–20
15 ☐ Matt. 15; Ps. 109:21–31
16 ☐ Matt. 16; Ps. 110

17 ☐ Matt. 17; Ps. 111
18 ☐ Matt. 18; Ps. 112
19 ☐ Matt. 19; Ps. 113
20 ☐ Matt. 20; Ps. 114
21 ☐ Matt. 21
22 ☐ Matt. 22
23 ☐ Matt. 23; Ps. 115
24 ☐ Matt. 24
25 ☐ Matt. 25
26 ☐ Matt. 26
27 ☐ Matt. 27
28 ☐ Matt. 28; Ps. 116
29 ☐ 2 Tim. 1; Ps. 117
30 ☐ Review

OCTOBER
1 ☐ 2 Tim. 2; Ps. 118
2 ☐ 2 Tim. 3; Ps. 119:1–24
3 ☐ 2 Tim. 4; Ps. 119:25–56
4 ☐ Titus 1; Ps. 119:57–80
5 ☐ Titus 2; Ps. 119:81–104
6 ☐ Titus 3; Ps. 119:105–136
7 ☐ Philem.; Ps. 119:137–160
8 ☐ Heb. 1; Ps. 119:161–176
9 ☐ Heb. 2; Ps. 120
10 ☐ Heb. 3; Ps. 121
11 ☐ Heb. 4; Ps. 122
12 ☐ Heb. 5; Ps. 123
13 ☐ Heb. 6; Ps. 124
14 ☐ Heb. 7; Ps. 125
15 ☐ Heb. 8; Ps. 126
16 ☐ Heb. 9; Ps. 127
17 ☐ Heb. 10; Ps. 128
18 ☐ Heb. 11
19 ☐ Heb. 12; Ps. 129
20 ☐ Heb. 13; Ps. 130
21 ☐ James 1; Ps. 131
22 ☐ James 2; Ps. 132
23 ☐ James 3; Ps. 133
24 ☐ James 4; Ps. 134
25 ☐ James 5; Ps. 135
26 ☐ 1 Pet. 1; Ps. 136
27 ☐ 1 Pet. 2; Ps. 137
28 ☐ 1 Pet. 3; Ps. 138
29 ☐ 1 Pet. 4; Ps. 139
30 ☐ 1 Pet. 5; Ps. 140
31 ☐ Review

NOVEMBER
1 ☐ 2 Pet. 1; Ps. 141
2 ☐ 2 Pet. 2; Ps. 142
3 ☐ 2 Pet. 3; Ps. 143
4 ☐ John 1
5 ☐ John 2; Ps. 144
6 ☐ John 3; Ps. 145
7 ☐ John 4
8 ☐ John 5

9 ☐ John 6
10 ☐ John 7
11 ☐ John 8
12 ☐ John 9
13 ☐ John 10
14 ☐ John 11
15 ☐ John 12
16 ☐ John 13; Ps. 146
17 ☐ John 14; Ps. 147
18 ☐ John 15; Ps. 148
19 ☐ John 16; Ps. 149
20 ☐ John 17; Ps. 150
21 ☐ John 18
22 ☐ John 19
23 ☐ John 20; Prov. 1
24 ☐ John 21; Prov. 2
25 ☐ 1 John 1; Prov. 3
26 ☐ 1 John 2; Prov. 4
27 ☐ 1 John 3; Prov. 5
28 ☐ 1 John 4; Prov. 6
29 ☐ 1 John 5; Prov. 7
30 ☐ Review

DECEMBER
1 ☐ 2 John; 3 John; Prov. 8
2 ☐ Jude; Prov. 9
3 ☐ Rev. 1; Prov. 10
4 ☐ Rev. 2; Prov. 11
5 ☐ Rev. 3; Prov. 12
6 ☐ Rev. 4; Prov. 13
7 ☐ Rev. 5; Prov. 14
8 ☐ Rev. 6; Prov. 15
9 ☐ Rev. 7; Prov. 16
10 ☐ Rev. 8; Prov. 17
11 ☐ Rev. 9; Prov. 18
12 ☐ Rev. 10; Prov. 19
13 ☐ Rev. 11; Prov. 20
14 ☐ Rev. 12; Prov. 21
15 ☐ Rev. 13; Prov. 22
16 ☐ Rev. 14; Prov. 23
17 ☐ Rev. 15; Prov. 24
18 ☐ Rev. 16; Prov. 25
19 ☐ Rev. 17; Prov. 26
20 ☐ Rev. 18; Prov. 27
21 ☐ Rev. 19; Prov. 28
22 ☐ Rev. 20; Prov. 29
23 ☐ Rev. 21; Prov. 30
24 ☐ Rev. 22; Prov. 31
25 ☐ Year Review Week
26 ☐ Year Review Week
27 ☐ Year Review Week
28 ☐ Year Review Week
29 ☐ Year Review Week
30 ☐ Year Review Week
31 ☐ Year Review Week

OLD TESTAMENT OPTION ONE:
THE LAW

JUNE
1 ☐ Gen. 1–2
2 ☐ Gen. 3–4
3 ☐ Gen. 5–6
4 ☐ Gen. 7–8
5 ☐ Gen. 9–10
6 ☐ Gen. 11–12
7 ☐ Gen. 13–14
8 ☐ Gen. 15–16
9 ☐ Gen. 17–18
10 ☐ Gen. 19–20
11 ☐ Gen. 21–23
12 ☐ Gen. 24
13 ☐ Gen. 25–26
14 ☐ Gen. 27
15 ☐ Gen. 28–29
16 ☐ Gen. 30
17 ☐ Gen. 31
18 ☐ Gen. 32–33
19 ☐ Gen. 34–35
20 ☐ Gen. 36–37
21 ☐ Gen. 38
22 ☐ Gen. 39
23 ☐ Gen. 40–41
24 ☐ Gen. 42
25 ☐ Gen. 43–44
26 ☐ Gen. 45–46
27 ☐ Gen. 47–48
28 ☐ Gen. 49
29 ☐ Gen. 50
30 ☐ Review

JULY
1 ☐ Ex. 1–2
2 ☐ Ex. 3–4
3 ☐ Ex. 5–6
4 ☐ Ex. 7–8
5 ☐ Ex. 9–10
6 ☐ Ex. 11–12
7 ☐ Ex. 13–14
8 ☐ Ex. 15–16
9 ☐ Ex. 17–18
10 ☐ Ex. 19–20
11 ☐ Ex. 21–22
12 ☐ Ex. 23–24
13 ☐ Ex. 25–26
14 ☐ Ex. 27–28
15 ☐ Ex. 29–30
16 ☐ Ex. 31–32
17 ☐ Ex. 33–34
18 ☐ Ex. 35–36
19 ☐ Ex. 37–38

20 ☐ Ex. 39–40
21 ☐ Lev. 1–3
22 ☐ Lev. 4–5
23 ☐ Lev. 6–7
24 ☐ Lev. 8
25 ☐ Lev. 9–10*
26 ☐ Lev. 16–17
27 ☐ Lev. 18–19
28 ☐ Lev. 20–21
29 ☐ Lev. 22–23
30 ☐ Lev. 24
31 ☐ Review

AUGUST
1 ☐ Lev. 25–26
2 ☐ Lev. 27
3 ☐ Num. 1–2
4 ☐ Num. 3–4
5 ☐ Num. 5–6
6 ☐ Num. 7–8
7 ☐ Num. 9–10
8 ☐ Num. 11–12
9 ☐ Num. 13–14
10 ☐ Num. 15–16
11 ☐ Num. 17–18
12 ☐ Num. 19–20
13 ☐ Num. 21–22
14 ☐ Num. 23–24
15 ☐ Num. 25–26
16 ☐ Num. 27–28
17 ☐ Num. 29–30
18 ☐ Num. 31–32
19 ☐ Num. 33–34
20 ☐ Num. 35–36
21 ☐ Deut. 1–3
22 ☐ Deut. 4–5
23 ☐ Deut. 6–7
24 ☐ Deut. 8–9
25 ☐ Deut. 10–11*
26 ☐ Deut. 26–27
27 ☐ Deut. 28–29
28 ☐ Deut. 30–31
29 ☐ Deut. 32–33
30 ☐ Deut. 34
31 ☐ Review

OLD TESTAMENT OPTION TWO:
HISTORY

JUNE
1 ☐ Josh. 1–2
2 ☐ Josh. 3–4
3 ☐ Josh. 5–6
4 ☐ Josh. 7–8

5 ☐ Josh. 9–10
6 ☐ Josh. 11–12*
7 ☐ Josh. 22–23
8 ☐ Josh. 24
9 ☐ Judg. 1
10 ☐ Judg. 2–3
11 ☐ Judg. 4–5
12 ☐ Judg. 6–7
13 ☐ Judg. 8
14 ☐ Judg. 9
15 ☐ Judg. 10–12
16 ☐ Judg. 13–14
17 ☐ Judg. 15–16
18 ☐ Judg. 17–19
19 ☐ Judg. 20–21
20 ☐ Ruth 1–2
21 ☐ Ruth 3–4
22 ☐ 1 Sam. 1–2
23 ☐ 1 Sam. 3–4
24 ☐ 1 Sam. 5–7
25 ☐ 1 Sam. 8–9
26 ☐ 1 Sam. 10–11
27 ☐ 1 Sam. 12–13
28 ☐ 1 Sam. 14
29 ☐ 1 Sam. 15–16
30 ☐ 1 Sam. 17

JULY
1 ☐ 1 Sam. 18–19
2 ☐ 1 Sam. 20
3 ☐ 1 Sam. 21–22
4 ☐ 1 Sam. 23–24
5 ☐ 1 Sam. 25
6 ☐ 1 Sam. 26–27
7 ☐ 1 Sam. 28–29
8 ☐ 1 Sam. 30–31
9 ☐ 2 Sam. 1–2
10 ☐ 2 Sam. 3–4
11 ☐ 2 Sam. 5–6
12 ☐ 2 Sam. 7–8
13 ☐ 2 Sam. 9–11
14 ☐ 2 Sam. 12–13
15 ☐ 2 Sam. 14–15
16 ☐ 2 Sam. 16–17
17 ☐ 2 Sam. 18–19
18 ☐ 2 Sam. 20–21
19 ☐ 2 Sam. 22
20 ☐ 2 Sam. 23–24
21 ☐ 1 Kings 1–2
22 ☐ 1 Kings 3–4
23 ☐ 1 Kings 5–6
24 ☐ 1 Kings 7
25 ☐ 1 Kings 8
26 ☐ 1 Kings 9–10
27 ☐ 1 Kings 11
28 ☐ 1 Kings 12–13

*denotes gap in Scripture passages

29 ☐ 1 Kings 14–15
30 ☐ 1 Kings 16–17
31 ☐ 1 Kings 18

AUGUST

1 ☐ 1 Kings 19–20
2 ☐ 1 Kings 21–22
3 ☐ 2 Kings 1–2
4 ☐ 2 Kings 3–4
5 ☐ 2 Kings 5–6
6 ☐ 2 Kings 7–8
7 ☐ 2 Kings 9–10
8 ☐ 2 Kings 11–12
9 ☐ 2 Kings 13–14
10 ☐ 2 Kings 15–16
11 ☐ 2 Kings 17–18
12 ☐ 2 Kings 19–20
13 ☐ 2 Kings 21–22
14 ☐ 2 Kings 23
15 ☐ 2 Kings 24
16 ☐ Ezra 1–2
17 ☐ Ezra 3–4
18 ☐ Ezra 5–6
19 ☐ Ezra 7–8
20 ☐ Ezra 9–10
21 ☐ Neh. 1–2
22 ☐ Neh. 3–4
23 ☐ Neh. 5–6
24 ☐ Neh. 7–8
25 ☐ Neh. 9–10
26 ☐ Neh. 11–12
27 ☐ Neh. 13–14
28 ☐ Est. 1–2
29 ☐ Est. 3–5
30 ☐ Est. 6–8
31 ☐ Est. 9–10

OLD TESTAMENT OPTION THREE:
PROPHETS

JUNE

1 ☐ Isa. 1–2
2 ☐ Isa. 3–4
3 ☐ Isa. 5–6
4 ☐ Isa. 7–8
5 ☐ Isa. 9–10
6 ☐ Isa. 11–13
7 ☐ Isa. 14–15
8 ☐ Isa. 16–18
9 ☐ Isa. 19–21
10 ☐ Isa. 22–23
11 ☐ Isa. 24–26
12 ☐ Isa. 27–28
13 ☐ Isa. 29–30

14 ☐ Isa. 31–33
15 ☐ Isa. 34–36
16 ☐ Isa. 37–38
17 ☐ Isa. 39–40
18 ☐ Isa. 41–42
19 ☐ Isa. 43–44
20 ☐ Isa. 45–47
21 ☐ Isa. 48–49
22 ☐ Isa. 50–52
23 ☐ Isa. 53–55
24 ☐ Isa. 56–58
25 ☐ Isa. 59–60
26 ☐ Isa. 61–63
27 ☐ Isa. 64–66
28 ☐ Jer. 1–2
29 ☐ Jer. 3–4
30 ☐ Review

JULY

1 ☐ Jer. 5–6
2 ☐ Jer. 7–8
3 ☐ Jer. 9–10
4 ☐ Jer. 11–12
5 ☐ Jer. 13–14
6 ☐ Jer. 15–16
7 ☐ Jer. 17–18
8 ☐ Jer. 19–21
9 ☐ Jer. 22–23
10 ☐ Jer. 24–25
11 ☐ Jer. 26–27
12 ☐ Jer. 28–29
13 ☐ Jer. 30–31
14 ☐ Jer. 32
15 ☐ Jer. 33–34
16 ☐ Jer. 35–36
17 ☐ Jer. 37–38
18 ☐ Jer. 39–40
19 ☐ Jer. 41–42
20 ☐ Jer. 43–44
21 ☐ Jer. 45–47
22 ☐ Jer. 48–49
23 ☐ Jer. 50
24 ☐ Jer. 51
25 ☐ Jer. 52
26 ☐ Lam. 1–2
27 ☐ Lam. 3
28 ☐ Lam. 4–5
29 ☐ Ezek. 1–2
30 ☐ Ezek. 3–4
31 ☐ Review

AUGUST

1 ☐ Ezek. 5–7
2 ☐ Ezek. 8–10
3 ☐ Ezek. 11–12
4 ☐ Ezek. 13–14

5 ☐ Ezek. 15–16
6 ☐ Ezek. 17–18
7 ☐ Ezek. 19–20
8 ☐ Ezek. 21–22
9 ☐ Ezek. 23
10 ☐ Ezek. 24–25
11 ☐ Ezek. 26
12 ☐ Ezek. 27
13 ☐ Ezek. 28–29
14 ☐ Ezek. 30–31
15 ☐ Ezek. 32–33
16 ☐ Ezek. 34–35
17 ☐ Ezek. 36–37
18 ☐ Ezek. 38–39
19 ☐ Ezek. 40
20 ☐ Ezek. 41–42
21 ☐ Ezek. 43–44
22 ☐ Ezek. 45–46
23 ☐ Ezek. 47–48
24 ☐ Dan. 1
25 ☐ Dan. 2
26 ☐ Dan. 3–4
27 ☐ Dan. 5–6
28 ☐ Dan. 7–8
29 ☐ Dan. 9–10
30 ☐ Dan. 11–12
31 ☐ Review

OLD TESTAMENT OPTION FOUR:
POETRY/MINOR PROPHETS

JUNE

1 ☐ Job 1–2
2 ☐ Job 3–4
3 ☐ Job 5–6
4 ☐ Job 7–8
5 ☐ Job 9–10
6 ☐ Job 11–12
7 ☐ Job 13–14
8 ☐ Job 15–16
9 ☐ Job 17–18
10 ☐ Job 19–20
11 ☐ Job 21–22
12 ☐ Job 23–24
13 ☐ Job 25–26
14 ☐ Job 27–28
15 ☐ Job 29–30
16 ☐ Job 31–32
17 ☐ Job 33–34
18 ☐ Job 35–36
19 ☐ Job 37–38
20 ☐ Job 39–40
21 ☐ Job 41–42

22	☐	Prov. 1
23	☐	Prov. 2
24	☐	Prov. 3
25	☐	Prov. 4
26	☐	Prov. 5
27	☐	Prov. 6
28	☐	Prov. 7
29	☐	Prov. 8
30	☐	Review

JULY

1	☐	Prov. 9
2	☐	Prov. 10
3	☐	Prov. 11
4	☐	Prov. 12
5	☐	Prov. 13
6	☐	Prov. 14
7	☐	Prov. 15
8	☐	Prov. 16
9	☐	Prov. 17
10	☐	Prov. 18
11	☐	Prov. 19
12	☐	Prov. 20
13	☐	Prov. 21
14	☐	Prov. 22
15	☐	Prov. 23
16	☐	Prov. 24
17	☐	Prov. 25
18	☐	Prov. 26
19	☐	Prov. 27
20	☐	Prov. 28
21	☐	Prov. 29
22	☐	Prov. 30
23	☐	Prov. 31
24	☐	Eccl. 1–3
25	☐	Eccl. 4–6
26	☐	Eccl. 7–9
27	☐	Eccl. 10–12
28	☐	Song 1–3
29	☐	Song 4–6
30	☐	Song 7–8
31	☐	Review

AUGUST

1	☐	Hos. 1–2
2	☐	Hos. 3–5
3	☐	Hos. 6–8
4	☐	Hos. 9–11
5	☐	Hos. 12–14
6	☐	Joel 1
7	☐	Joel 2
8	☐	Joel 3
9	☐	Amos 1–2
10	☐	Amos 3–4
11	☐	Amos 5–6
12	☐	Amos 7–8
13	☐	Amos 9
14	☐	Obad.
15	☐	Jon. 1–2
16	☐	Jon. 3–4
17	☐	Mic. 1–2
18	☐	Mic. 3–4
19	☐	Mic. 5–7
20	☐	Nah. 1–3
21	☐	Hab. 1–3
22	☐	Zeph. 1–2
23	☐	Hag. 1–2
24	☐	Zech. 1–3
25	☐	Zech. 4–6
26	☐	Zech. 7–9
27	☐	Zech. 10–12
28	☐	Zech. 13–14
29	☐	Mal. 1–2
30	☐	Mal. 3–4
31	☐	Review

APPENDIX C
GUIDE TO **DAILY TIME** WITH **GOD**

Step 1: Pause

Spend a few moments in prayer, asking the Holy Spirit to guide and direct your reading of the Bible. Read with an open heart and listen for any words of direction, encouragement, or correction.

Step 2: Read

Go over the reading plan and read the chapters of the Bible listed for that day. While you read, underline or highlight any words, phrases, or verses that you sense God is speaking to you about.

Step 3: Write

Turn to a fresh page in your journal, write the date and page number at the top, and then go through the four-step process of journaling to reflect your thoughts.

- **First,** write out the verse or passage of Scripture that the Holy Spirit has shown you for that day. Include the reference.
- **Second,** look at the surrounding context of the verse you selected and write down any observations. Try to explain the passage in your own words.
- **Third,** ask how this verse might apply to your life. What is God calling you to do or to remember as a result? What is your next step and how can you be obedient?
- **Fourth,** write out a closing prayer. Use this final section to speak back to God a request or commitment.

Finish your journal entry by giving it a short title at the top and then transfer the date, Scripture reference, title, and page number to the table of contents.

Step 4: Review

When you finish your journal entry, review the accountability questions from the Discipleship Group Agenda, located on the inside front cover of the *Banding Together Journal*.

Step 5: Pray

Conclude your time by praying for what you have written and for anyone who needs to surrender to God.

APPENDIX D
TEN **FREQUENTLY ASKED** QUESTIONS

---

1. What kind of journal should I use?

We have created the *Banding Together Journal* as a companion guide to this resource. It contains the reading plan, discipleship group agenda, prayer notes, journaling process, and several months' worth of journal entry pages.

2. What if someone in the group doesn't like to journal?

Start small by inviting them to simply write out the verse of Scripture they highlighted and jot a few bullet points. The most important part of the process is hearing from God.

3. How long should a discipleship group meet before multiplying?

Discipleship groups ought to meet at least twelve months before multiplying. However, it is suggested that at eighteen to twenty-four months, group members should be identifying new people they can disciple.

4. Can someone stay in their existing discipleship group if they decide to multiply?

Yes. In fact, multiplication often works best if the person stays in their existing group for a season of time while launching a new group until it becomes established.

5. Are discipleship groups designed to take the place of traditional small groups?

Not necessarily. In my church context, we found the need for a separate mixed-gender small group environment for building friendships, practicing hospitality, and reaching our community. We call those community groups. They meet less frequently than discipleship groups and serve a different purpose.

6. Can this model work with students and children?

Absolutely. In fact, we are in the process of developing other resources and a modified reading plan that can be used with students and children as well.

7. What should I do with an inconsistent discipleship group member?

First, be sure to set the pace by prioritizing every group meeting and showing up prepared. Your consistency as a leader is vital. Second, remind group members of the importance of gathering together. Third, if a group member continues to miss meetings, find a gracious way to address the issue and offer them the option of leaving the group for a season.

8. How can I get my group to share during the accountability portion of the group?

Time and transparency. As a leader, you will need to set the pace and practice vulnerability and openness. It takes time for trust to be established. It might be wise, as you first begin your group, to focus the accountability on obedience to the Bible reading.

9. Are there any requirements for leading a discipleship group?

Leaders must be followers of Christ and seeking to walk in obedience to his commands. Ideally, they should also participate in a training that models the discipleship group process. Group discipleship is different than mentoring or a teacher-student model, and the greatest requirement is a growing relationship with Christ and commitment to obedience.

10. Do you recommend supplementing discipleship groups with any other type of biblical instruction?

Sunday school, inductive Bible studies, online instruction, and other classes or seminars can certainly be helpful aids to making more and better disciples. However, these options don't often emphasize multiplication and won't sustain a long-term movement of disciple making. In offering other modes of instruction, always stay focused on building the structure of discipleship groups.

NOTES

Introduction

1. Francis Chan, *Multiply: Disciples Making Disciples* (Colorado Springs: David C. Cook, 2012), 27.
2. John Piper, "I Will Not Be a Velvet-Mouthed Preacher," Desiring God Conference, 2009, https://www.desiringgod.org/messages/i-will-not-be-a-velvet-mouthed-preacher.
3. Arnold A. Dallimore, *George Whitefield: God's Anointed Servant in the Great Revival of the Eighteenth Century* (Wheaton, IL: Crossway Books, 1990), 195.
4. John Wigger, *American Saint: Francis Asbury and the Methodists* (New York: Oxford University Press, 2009), 3.
5. Steve Addison, *Movements that Change the World: Five Keys to Spreading the Gospel* (Downers Grove, IL: InterVarsity Press, 2011), 87.
6. Robby Gallaty, *Rediscovering Discipleship: Making Jesus' Final Words Our First Work* (Grand Rapids, MI: Zondervan, 2015), 115.
7. Gallaty, *Rediscovering Discipleship*, 115.
8. John Wesley, "Journal," *The Works of John Wesley*, vol. 3, (Peabody, MA: Hendrickson Publishers, 1984), 144.
9. Leonidas Rosser, *Class Meetings: Embracing Their Origin, Nature, Obligation, and Benefits* (Richmond, VA: Self-Published, 1855), 178.
10. Alan Hirsch, *Disciplism: Reimagining Evangelism Through the Lens of Discipleship* (Exponential Resources, 2014), 19.

11. See www.wesleyan.org/about.
12. Mike Breen, "Why the Missional Movement Will Fail," http://www.vergenetwork.org/2011/09/14/mike-breen-why-the-missional-movement-will-fail/.
13. Assumes three to the tenth power.
14. C.S. Lewis, *The Problem of Pain* (New York: HarperCollins, 2001), 91.
15. Oxford Living Dictionaries, "practical," https://en.oxforddictionaries.com/definition/practical.

Part One
1. James Clear, "Vince Lombardi on the Hidden Power of Mastering the Fundamentals," Huffington Post, December 6, 2017, https://www.huffingtonpost.com/james-clear/vince-lombardi-on-the-hid_b_9306782.html.
2. "Super Bowl I," Wikipedia, https://en.wikipedia.org/wiki/Super_Bowl_I.
3. *Remember the Titans*, dir. Boaz Yakin, DVD (USA: Walt Disney Studios Home Entertainment, 2007).
4. Kevin M. Watson, *The Class Meeting: Reclaiming a Forgotten (and Essential) Small Group Experience* (Wilmore, KY: Seedbed Publishing, 2014), 8.
5. Wayne Cordeiro, *The Divine Mentor: Growing Your Faith as You Sit at the Feet of the Savior* (Bloomington, MN: Bethany House Publishing, 2007), 40.
6. Eugene H. Peterson, *A Long Obedience in the Same Direction* (Downers Grove, IL: InterVarsity Press, 2000), 17.
7. *Merriam-Webster Dictionary*, "discipline," https://www.merriam-webster.com/dictionary/discipline.
8. Nick Harrison, *Walking with Wesley: A Ninety-Day Devotional* (Indianapolis, IN: Wesleyan Publishing House, 2014), 51.

Part Two
1. Robert E. Coleman, *The Master Plan of Evangelism* (Grand Rapids, MI: Baker Book House, 1994), 27.
2. Ray VanderLaan and *Follow the Rabbi Ministries*.
3. Neil Cole, "A Perspective on the Parable of the Soils," CMA Resources, November 23, 2010, https://www.cmaresources.org/article/a-perspective-on-the-parable-of-the-soils_neil-cole.
4. Mark L. Gorveatte, *Lead Like Wesley: Help for Today's Ministry Servants* (Indianapolis, IN: Wesleyan Publishing House, 2016), 23.

5. Mark Benjamin, Matt LeRoy, and J.D. Walt, *Wake Up: An Introduction to the Second Half of the Gospel* (Franklin, TN: Seedbed Publishing, 2017), vii.

6. Kevin M. Watson and Scott T. Kisker, *The Band Meeting: Rediscovering Relational Discipleship in Transformational Community* (Franklin, TN: Seedbed Publishing, 2017), 109.

7. Gallaty, *Rediscovering Discipleship*, 148.

8. Cordeiro, *The Divine Mentor*, 102.

9. Watson and Kisker, *The Band Meeting*, 7.

10. Watson and Kisker, *The Band Meeting*, 7.

11. Watson and Kisker, *The Band Meeting*, 10.

12. Charles Wesley, "O for a Thousand Tongues to Sing," *Sing Joyfully Hymnal* (Carol Stream, IL: Tabernacle Publishing Company, 1989), 93.

13. Watson and Kisker, *The Band Meeting*, 13.

14. Dave Ferguson and Jon Ferguson, *Finding Your Way Back to God: 5 Awakenings to Your New Life* (Colorado Springs: Multnomah Books, 2015), 12.

15. Hirsch, *Disciplism*, 25.

16. Bobby Harrington and Greg Wiens, *Becoming a Disciple Maker: The Pursuit of Level 5 Disciple Making* (Discipleship.org Resources, 2017), 21.

Part Three

1. C. Peter Wagner, *Church Planting for a Greater Harvest: A Comprehensive Guide* (Ventura, CA: Regal Books, 1990), 11.

2. Todd Wilson and Dave Ferguson, *Becoming a Level Five Multiplying Church Field Guide* (Exponential Resources, 2015), 38.

3. Wilson and Ferguson, *Becoming a Level Five Multiplying Church Field Guide*, 45.

4. http://www.beamezion.org/resources/leadership/Connecting EmpoweringLeadership.pdf.

5. Todd Wilson, *Dream Big, Plan Smart: Finding Your Pathway to Level 5 Multiplication* (Exponential Resources, 2016), 57.

6. Augustus Strong, *Systematic Theology: Volume 3—The Doctrine of Salvation* (Philadelphia: American Baptist Publication Society, 1909), 871.

7. Watson and Kisker, *The Band Meeting*, 90.

8. John H. Wigger, *Taking Heaven by Storm: Methodism and the Rise of Popular Christianity in America* (New York: Oxford University Press, 1998), 94.

9. Addison, *Movements that Change the World*, 117.

Conclusion

1. Watson and Kisker, *The Band Meeting*, 95.
2. https://www.encountertrinity.com/about/vision-values/.
3. C.S. Lewis, *Mere Christianity* (New York: HarperCollins, 2001), 199.
4. Dietrich Bonhoeffer, *The Cost of Discipleship* (New York: Touchstone, 1995), 59.
5. David Garrison, *Church Planting Movements: How God is Redeeming a Lost World* (Midlothian, VA: Wig Take Resources, 2004).
6. Peter F. Drucker, *Managing Oneself* (Boston: Harvard Business Review Press, 2017), 3.
7. *Oxford Living Dictionary,* "commission," https://en.oxford dictionaries.com/definition/commission.